Presented To:

_____

From:

_____

Date:

_____

Books That Enrich You
To Enrich Others

Books that bless the heart and soothe the soul. Whether you are seeking to invest a little something into your personal development, or whether you simply need a shot of inspiration to fuel your aspirations.

Open Scroll Publications offers a new breed of books designed to impact the mind, touch the heart, and ignite the spirit.

SURVIVING

SPIRITUAL ABUSE

Hope, healing and restoration
for those who have
experienced hurt

Francesca McDowall

Published by Open Scroll Publications

Copyright © 2021 by Francesca McDowall

Visit: www.survivingspiritualabuse.com

Email: info@survivingspiritualabuse.com

Join our community on Facebook and Instagram @ssa.restart

First published 2021 by:
Open Scroll Publications Ltd,
Kemp House, 160 City Road,
London, EC1V 2NX.
www.openscroll.co.uk

ISBN: 978-1-9999856-4-6

A CIP catalogue record of this book is available from the British Library.

Cover design and Typeset by Open Scroll Publications.

Printed in Great Britain.

Dedication

This book is dedicated to those who have been hurt, neglected, abused and rejected. Your resilience, tenacity and inner determination to survive is phenomenal. Healing and wholeness are woven into your destiny.

Acknowledgements

Firstly, I would like to acknowledge my Lord and Saviour Jesus Christ who provides the meaning, foundation and reason for my existence. I am grateful that I was introduced to my faith as a child. I want to thank my wonderful family, both biological and spiritual, who are incredibly supportive and understanding. You cheer me on and provide emotional, practical and spiritual stability and for that I am thankful.

To 'Ohana' the friends who have become family I love and appreciate your care and consistency over the years.

Pastors Michael & Katrina, you have taught me fundamental truths of leadership just by being yourselves. Thank you for teaching me what Godly leadership looks like and for lovingly challenging me to grow.

To my church family, TLC, God bless you. I have experienced so much agape from you all. To Sister Ulite, Mary and the Bible Study family thank you for providing a safe and secure space in which I could grow.

Love and blessings to 'Released to Worship' my dance family who have nurtured and taught me commitment. The laughter, tears, worship and prayer we shared hold a dear place in my heart.

Pastor Paul and Pastor Stanley, my spiritual mentors who continually pray for me, encourage me and cover me, thank you. To those who have counselled me both formally and informally, thank you. You were heavens mouthpiece and helped remould my mind-set towards truth.

Sincerest thank you to my incredible mother Angela McDowall who spent hours and hours assisting with the editing process. You are greatly appreciated. A huge thank you also goes to my brother in Christ, Marcel White, who proofread the final manuscript. Your advice and feedback has been invaluable.

Lastly a special thank you to the courageous individuals, who shared their survival stories, though your real names have not been used in this book, heaven records them and I am truly grateful.

Contents

Foreward

I would like to begin this foreword with an apology.

To all those brave souls who have somehow managed to garner the courage to tell their stories in this book, please accept my sincerest apologies for what you have had to endure. Also to those reading this book with similar accounts of hurt and harm through the abuse of power at the hands of a Minister ... may the healing balm of the Holy Spirit wash over you even as you begin to read this divinely-timed publication.

There really are no words to begin to reconcile in our minds why these kinds of atrocities can happen in the most sacred of all grounds. But what I will say is that those who may appear to start out as victims in these kinds of scenarios, often end up as life's greatest victors. Far from being destroyed, those who receive a healing touch from our heavenly Father, can be seen emerging from these horrendous experiences stronger, wiser and more discerning than ever before. By their own accounts, they become far more equipped to identify, help and support others on a similar journey. And, although this may seem like a very small consolation, I still feel that it's worth a mention.

Now, there are two reasons why I endorse, and highly recommend this book. The first, is because in my 28 years of serving as a Minister of the Gospel, I have yet to come across a more effective book on the topic of Spiritual Abuse. Although it is not an exhaustive work on the topic per se, something about the way it combines personal testimonials (from such a wide range of individuals) with the most insightful of teachings by the author, makes it a **must have** in any ministry collection.

This will become one of my 'staples' as I minister to those who have been affected by this awful, and often faceless form of abuse.

My second reason for recommending this book is because of the author, Francesca. They say that hurting people, hurt people; but whole people heal people. Watching Francesca's journey has been a magnificent display of what the Word of God teaches in Romans 8:28-29:

> *And we know that God causes everything to work together for the good of those who love God and are called according to his purpose for them. For God knew his people in advance, and he chose them to become like his Son, so that his Son would be the firstborn among many brothers and sisters.*

Romans 8:28-29 NLT

There are very few people that I know who are a better embodiment of God's grace on a life than the author. Her courage, wisdom, diligence, and heart for others, makes her the perfect conduit for the Lord to flow through to bring healing and deliverance.

If you've ever been hurt in a church setting before (*and there's no hurt like church hurt*), you are holding the antidote in your hands. May the Lord bless, restore and empower you as you allow the author to take you on a journey of restoration.

Michael Ekwulugo

Senior Pastor of The Transformation life Centre,
Birmingham, UK
Author of *It's Your Time*
(*Your Generation Awaits You*)

A Letter To The Reader

Seek ye first the kingdom of God and His righteousness,
and all these things will be added unto you.

Mathew 6:33 KJV

I met the author several years ago. Fran was introduced to me by a young person at my church. I had started on my own journey of finding out more about dance in the bible, and had started to share my joy and passion with others who felt the same harmony to dance before the Lord. We gathered together and I facilitated weekly worship dance training sessions, and Fran started to attend.

Immediately, during these sessions I saw something in Fran that I felt she had pushed aside; her leadership skills and creativity. Each week she would hold back and politely excuse herself from the next dance practice. I couldn't understand why, but I would never acknowledge that it was her last time at dance practice. Although she appeared uncomfortable and was unable to fully and freely express herself in dance and movement, she returned weekly. This was until the weight of the 'chains' came off.

After reading this awesome book, it all makes sense. The introduction summarised for me some of the gaps and silences along the journey of our friendship. Fran's inability to trust or believe that genuine care existed.

The pages of this book opens up the pain of spiritual abuse. Rejection from a shepherd whose primary responsibility was to look out for the safety and welfare of His sheep.

Personally I had mixed feelings while reading, mainly one of empathy while scanning the pages of this unknown area of Fran's past experiences.

I am overwhelmed by her creativity in writing and her ability to draw out painful emotions, replacing them with emotions from a place of deeper love for Gods compassion. His love that covers and protects.

The heart is deceitful above all things,
and desperately wicked, who can know it?
Jeremiah 17:9 KJV.

The Bible speaks of the "heart" the ruling centre of man's desire. The heart of a true believer is to pray daily for diligence, true healing and purification for the body of believers.

Reading this book reminds me of the place where many come to ministries for healing, but instead walk away with war scars. It's like unidentified bruises that were not seen before a person went to bed; but woke up to find themselves black and blue.

My early years as a new Christian connected me to Fran's experience of manipulation from the pulpit, and I am reminded that in everything there is a season. I received joy from turning the pages, as it unveiled that this is indeed a book of hope; a reflection of forgiveness and courageousness in this journey of sharing.

I have witnessed Fran's commitment to excellence. She is a strong supportive leader, having a firm foundation in Jesus Christ.

'Seek first kingdom principles' is the flavour of this book. It demonstrates how we acknowledge people who have hurt us knowingly or unknowingly. Whilst reading you are able to navigate through a sense of Godly love and do not wish to seek any form of revenge. My thoughts are, that this is the heart of a true worshipper one who demonstrates forgiveness. Fran's heart's desire is to do the will of God, and that which is right in the eyes of God. We must always start by forgiving the person in the mirror.

I witness many women who care for others; issue the prescribed medicine to others, but will not take the recommended dose for themselves. Read the label and take a spoonful. I am reminded of the scriptures:

> *I shall not die, but live, and declare the works of the Lord.*
>
> Psalm 118:17 KJV

And that:

> *...weeping may endure for a night,*
> *but joy cometh in the morning.*
>
> Psalm 30:5b KJV

Isaiah 60 : 1 starts with:

> *Arise, shine; for thy light is come, and the glory of*
> *the Lord is risen upon thee...*
>
> Isaiah 60:1 KJV

This is a reminder of the transformation that can come for those who follow the ways of the Lord.

This book teaches that whilst for many 'hope' may be to keep things to yourself, or live with the pain hoping it will get better; it is not the truth! Some things must be vomited up, even though finding someone you trust isn't easy, as we know Bishops and Pastors have not always demonstrated the greatest integrity.

Fran unveiling her truth of physical and emotional abuse through the pages of this book, demonstrates the virtue of a woman who has overcome fear and trauma to empower others, through life coaching, ministry in dance and unspoken words. Through it all Fran has held on to the fact that God has a greater plan.

I would encourage anyone who has experienced spiritual abuse to read this book. It doesn't demonstrate an eye for an eye, it demonstrates being anchored in the one that created you. Trusting in a heavenly father who heals, comforts and nurtures. The one who heals the wounds of life and brings restoration. These may just sound like beautiful words, but nevertheless they speak truth. Over the years I have witnessed Fran's pain, tears and her joy, sometimes all in one day. This isn't an easy road, it takes years and sometimes you wonder where you will end up. I encourage you to get to the end of your book. The road always starts somewhere. Your journey is not about where you have come from, it is about where you are going.

Helen Keller stated that: *"only through the experience of trials and suffering can the soul be strengthened, ambitious inspired and success achieved"*

I thank you Fran for stepping behind your veil and holding the hands of others who may have been paralysed by fear, trauma and abuse not recognising their worth and angry at God when they did all that was right. You are a true Kingdom Ambassador.

I pray the words on these pages will breathe life into every reader's life.

Claudeth Bennett

Founder and Director of Released to Worship Dance Ministry, Regional Chair of NLDN, Business Owner holding a Certificate in Education and Ambassador of the Kingdom.

Introduction

*D*ear Reader,

Thank you for picking up this book. There are thousands of books you could have chosen to read, but the fact you are reading these words, at this time, I believe is significant. I have prayed for you, and I look forward to our journey together through the pages of this book as the stories unfold.

To really get to know another person I believe there has to be a certain level of transparency and honesty, and for that reason I must start with a confession. Not so long ago I hated leadership! I mean, I really hated it. I categorically did not believe in the concept, pattern and examples of leadership in the church and certainly did not trust it. Pastors, Elders, Deacons whatever you called them, I had no respect, no care and absolutely no belief in the notion of leadership in a faith context!

Apologies if you are in any form of leadership, I am too, but bear with me as I explain. You see I had not always held this viewpoint, but over the year's painful life events had occurred and they slowly but assuredly changed me. Thankfully the hatred is no longer a reality in my life, Jesus has healed my heart, but I wanted you to know where I am coming from.

I grew up in a stable, loving family and regularly attended a local charismatic church. I was saved at the tender age of 14, baptised and filled with the Holy Spirit about a year later when I was 15. As youth we were encouraged in our personal relationship with Christ, we had regular cell, or small group meetings, as well as youth services. Our summers were spent attending Soul Survivor, a large 5-day youth conference, where we camped and spent our evenings gathered with thousands of others in worship services. At my church I became a cell group leader when I was about 16, and also the leader of the Christian Union at my all girls High School. As a teenager the faith leaders around me nourished and nurtured my emerging leadership gifts and qualities, and also provided the necessary support to remain grounded. I remember having regular catch ups with the youth leaders who provided guidance and wisdom. It was a solid start, and I love that hindsight provides a beautiful lens through which I can look at my past and see it for the richness that it was. Of course there were the usual amounts of hiccups and challenges which we all know is normal along this journey called life. However, through it all, I am thankful for the beginnings of my faith.

Everything changed when I became a young adult, left home and went to university. I started attending a different church, that was different in its doctrines, different in its culture, different in its belief systems and different in the way the leaders pastored, and 'took care' of their congregation. That is where I started to encounter things that just didn't seem quite right. There were certain behaviour, actions and words that at that time I had no reference or language for, this was to come later.

As you read this book you will learn and hear of my journey along with the stories of others who are survivors of spiritual abuse. I think for many people, the term 'spiritual abuse' is not one they are familiar with, or maybe a term connected to something that happened, or is happening to them. I know I certainly didn't. Firstly, because I did not see there was anything 'wrong' happening to me and around me. Secondly because I had never heard of the term, and thirdly because we can often think, '*if anything goes wrong maybe we are partly to blame.*' I will explain the definition of spiritual abuse, and how it shares similarities with other forms of abuse further on.

It is important to note that the inspiration for this book was to provide an answer to sometimes unanswered questions. It is also to let other survivors know that they are not alone and to help unpick this complex, unspoken of, and clearly misunderstood type of abuse. It is to provide hope, healing and restoration. I chose not to share names of organisations, churches or individuals in this book because it is not about exposing them, but exposing the spirit that works through them. It is not about bashing leaders or churches, and the real life case studies that have been shared also do not name organisations, churches or individuals for these same reasons. I felt that it was important to hear from different people, and also illustrate the different forms in which this abuse can take place. Incidentally there were many more stories that I could have included, as the number of people who have experienced some form of spiritual abuse is quite alarming.

As you are reading, I would encourage you to take the necessary time to reflect and pray as you feel appropriate. Information is great, but with my Coaching hat on, I would strongly advocate the importance of implementation. This principal is founded in the Bible in the book of James 1:22 The scripture says:

But be doers of the word, and not hearers only, deceiving yourselves.
James 1:22 NKJV

Another version explains it this way:

> *Don't just listen to the Word of Truth and not respond to it,*
> *for that is the essence of self-deception. So always let his*
> *Word become like poetry written and fulfilled by your life!*
>
> James 1:22 TPT

If any part of this book triggers something in you, it may mean there are areas in your own life, own history or present situation that have not yet been fully dealt with. I would really encourage you to invite the Holy Spirit, and partner with Him to take you a journey that will bring you into healing, restoration and liberty. We each have the assurance that freedom is possible. The book of John teaches:

> *Then Jesus said to those Jews who believed Him, "If you abide*
> *in My word, you are My disciples indeed. And you shall*
> *know the truth, and the truth shall make you free."*
>
> John 8:31-32 KJV

To other survivors, whether recognised, acknowledged or not, I commend you. My prayer for you is that any identity that is not yours will be stripped away, and that you would be free to live solely in the identity, acceptance and love of Christ and your stature in Him.

To the curious, because let's be honest there are some who will read this book to hear my story, maybe because you know me in some capacity, or because this topic is completely new. Either way you are warmly invited along this journey. My hope and prayer for you is that you will be awakened to the wider issues of spiritual abuse, how strong survivors are and also the importance of servant leadership. To the curious who have simply never heard of spiritual abuse or are new to the faith you are also welcome. I pray your discernment is increased as you learn what can happen in a faith context, and understand that due to the futility of mankind even Christians can misrepresent a perfect God. I pray you will be further determined to seek excellence in all things kingdom related.

To leaders, I pray you will have deeper revelation of servant leadership as the roadmap for Kingdom living. I pray you will seek the Father as to any areas in which you may need to develop and grow. I pray your heart would remain attentive to the Fathers heart, and align accordingly. The word of God is indeed a mirror. May you reflect more of Christ as you serve His children through your leadership.

To the leaders, who have been, or are currently perpetrators of spiritual abuse >sigh< ... there is room at the table. Whether it is known or unknown that your behaviour, words and actions are/were abusive and abhorrent to the Father, there is deliverance, change and mercy after repentance. May your heart be softened, and may you see the souls you serve through the eyes of a Sovereign God; through the eyes of a fiercely faithful Father who exemplifies a good, true Shepherd, who did indeed lay down His life for His sheep.

This book is a story of hope, triumph and victory after helplessness, tragedy and victimhood. Remain encouraged as you come along on this journey.

CHAPTER ONE

A Promising Start

Several years ago ... somewhere in the UK.

I glanced at the clock, it was 8:45pm, church service would be finishing soon, but the atmosphere was still charged. At the altar there were church brethren in tears, praying in tongues and also receiving prayer ministry. The sounds of deliverance rang throughout the pews and it felt like God was right there in the building. I saw and experienced things at this church, which we'll call 'Eden House' that I had never seen anywhere ... it felt like God was right there in the midst and it was captivating.

At every service 'something' would happen. Demons could often be seen manifesting as they threw, quite literally, members of the congregation off their chairs, in the aisles and at the altar. The congregation were told to clap their hands and pray for those going through deliverance. I remember seeing people roll on the floor from one side of the church to the other, as the ministers were seen violently casting out those spirits.

There would often be testimonies of deliverance, healing, miracles and breakthrough as we witnessed people's lives change, right in front of our eyes. This happened month after month, year after year and really was the heartbeat and focus of the church. There were visiting ministers who would come and hold conferences, often for the entire week, and again people would receive prophecy, prayer and healing. We would hear preaching that would have you standing up, hollering and clapping as you "received" the promises of God declared over your life. It was an incredible experience. At the time I remember feeling pleased and excited that I was fortunate enough to be a part of Eden House.

In the beginning I lived for those services. It was truly the highlight of my week. My life comprised of work, home and church and I thought this was so amazing. We were told all these things that happened at Eden House were a sign of the "anointing" … symbolic of the manifest presence of God, and this became a bit of a fix. "To feel the anointing" and "see something happen." I based a lot of my faith on these feelings and experiences.

Very often, in life, there are elements of truth mixed in with deception, and it wouldn't be a fair representation if I did not mention that Eden House was making an impact in the lives of families and the community. There would be events for the youth, mission trips and very practical support for families in need. Help and hope were offered and received by many different people. I loved, served and committed to being there, even sacrificing time and special occasions with own family, because I was all in, believing that I was serving God.

One aspect of Eden House that occurs in many other churches and Christian organisations was the aspect of financial giving; sowing, pledging and support! Giving is indeed a biblical principle and it is definitely a blessing to give to the work of the Lord and to sow into ministries. Sowing and reaping is also a biblical principle, and was stringently encouraged at most Eden House services. Paying tithes, giving offering and special gifts were an integral part of the culture. I personally experienced some incredible breakthroughs and answers to prayer from sowing for which I am grateful.

Whilst on the surface everything at Eden House seemed amazing and we were experiencing blessings, favour and the mighty hand of God. There came a time, however, when increasingly I had thoughts that 'something just didn't feel right.' Have you ever lived through a situation where something, somewhere was off, but you couldn't quite put your finger on it? It's not as if you could categorically say x,y,z happened or was wrong, but there was a sense of disingenuousness. I also saw how some other members and leaders were spoken about and treated and again something there felt 'off.'

Subconsciously I began to wonder and ask myself many questions relating to Eden House:

♦ Why after months and months, even years of 'deliverance' were some people still not free?

♦ What would happen if you couldn't pay, pledge or sow the suggested amount to secure God's blessing?

♦ If Eden House was unlike any other church in the region, as God was only ministering to people there, does that mean every other church was doing something wrong?

♦ Why did there have to be over 5 services a week, every week?

♦ How many more generational curses needed to be broken off the same people after years of praying?

- Is honouring someone's anointing over their character really the most important thing?

- Why did it seem like when some of these big visiting preachers stepped off the stage they appeared to be very different to the man that appeared on the pulpit?

- How much money was actually needed to be raised for the building fund? And why did the building never actually materialize?

- If the pastor was the only one really hearing God where does that leave the rest of us?

- Why were the members and leaders discouraged publicly from visiting other churches?

The questions and ponderings continued. If I did query anything directly with the leaders, which did not sit well with me, it felt like I was immediately shut down. I recall sharing that I wasn't comfortable to deliver a short teaching with the church as I had been instructed to because I couldn't verify the source of the information. Well who told me to question the Pastor. My response to what I was asked to do was taken as demonstration that I clearly had an attitude and was being difficult! When you begin to see a pattern of negative responses to your questions and queries you quickly learn that it is better to keep quiet, rather than rock the boat and be deemed rebellious.

I am in no way saying that every component in my list of questions demonstrates that something is wrong, but collectively they painted a picture that something was indeed very wrong. But when everyone else around you is joyfully living out their faith at Eden House, and it's become the only Christian fellowship place you've been part of in years, it became easier and more comfortable to conclude it must just have been me, and carry on as normal.

Relationships in churches, like in most families, can often be complex. An interesting mix of love, support, co-dependency, differing forms of attachment, and at times toxicity. And yet there is also security and comfort in the familiar. The dichotomy of commitment and concern can often result in insecurity, confusion, underlying fear and anxiety.

We will not be addressing the answers to all my questions in this book, but it has to be recognised, and for some an education in the fact that for many individuals who find themselves in a spiritually abusive environment it is rarely a simple or straight forward matter. Whether you leave, stay or raise concerns there are always mixed emotions. For many it is the underlying loyalty to the church and fear of what might happen if they do make a decision to leave which brings the greatest confusion. Possibly, it may have been drummed into them for years that 'this is the place where God is', and the prospect of leaving such a place can be overwhelmingly frightening. They would be without the covering of that particular place, or dare I say, "without God." After all, they may have been warned, sorry told, "…a genuine believer would never want to leave the place where the heavens are open and where God is pouring His blessing, favour, healing and anointing…"

Additionally, the nature of toxic or spiritually abusive church environments is that dependency has been so embedded in the culture that the thought of being without the leading, guiding and 'support' of the leadership is frightening. For some it may even be unthinkable. This has been their lifeline, source, oxygen mask, albeit counterfeit, but who knows what living outside this environment would look like?

Too often we judge what we do not understand, and there are many similarities with other forms of abuse in how an individual is impacted and affected by spiritual abuse. Let's now start at the end and work our way backwards, as we explore exactly what spiritual abuse is.

Chapter Two

What Is Spiritual Abuse And Is It In The Bible?

What Is Spiritual Abuse?

*F*irstly, let's look at what constitutes abuse. The term 'abuse' in its simplest form in relation to people, is the use of someone to bad effect or for a bad purpose. In other words, it is the misuse and ill-treatment of someone. In the UK it is commonly recognised that there are four main types of abuse that people experience; physical, sexual, neglect and emotional abuse. However, there are many more identified categories of abuse including verbal abuse, financial abuse, bullying, psychological trauma and domestic abuse. As this book focuses on adults, we will not venture into the varying types of child abuse, however in whatever manner abuse takes place let me be very clear it is wrong. There can often be legal ramifications and it is abhorrent to heaven.

Spiritual Abuse can be understood in several ways. And whilst spiritual abuse may take place in other faith communities, as a Christian and in the context of this book my definition of spiritual abuse is any form of abuse occurring as a result of being in, or connected to the Christian faith, and/or from one Christian (individual, group, organisation) to another. The types of abuse may range from emotional, physical, sexual, financial to psychological.

In addition, the spiritual abuse could also manifest as intimidation, manipulation, gaslighting (psychological manipulation in which one person or a group spread doubt, causing the victim to doubt their sanity, memory, judgment or understanding), turning others against you, using scriptures out of context for personal gain, coercive control, mind control, brain washing and witchcraft. This list is not extensive, and there may be other ways in which someone perpetuates spiritual abuse. Spiritual abuse is often carried out by, but not limited to, someone in a position of leadership, power or authority toward someone that they lead.

Spiritual abuse, like all others forms of abuse, does not discriminate, and can be found across all church denominations, cultures, races, ethnicities, social demographic groupings and geographical locations. Spiritual abuse also does not discriminate across age or gender. Perpetrators can be both men and women, and survivors can also be men and women. I have no statistical data to evidence my thoughts, however from the many individuals I have spoken to and accounts that I am aware of, it appears that the main perpetrators of spiritual abuse are men and the majority of victims, or survivors are women. I think it is also important to note that when it comes to reporting abuse there are often societal, and cultural pressures that may hinder and prevent as many men coming forward to report incidents. I believe this is also a contributing factor on the gender breakdown for known cases of spiritual abuse, that being said there may be just as many men that experience this as women.

The title of this book was inspired by the Holy Spirit, rather than one that I choose, although I do feel the term surviving is absolutely appropriate, as surviving means to continue to exist, remain alive and or remain intact. Therefore 'surviving' spiritual abuse is not necessarily only referring to the moments and incidents in which the abuse or ill treatment actually took place. But surviving also refers to the after effects which may include:

- The emotional and psychological damage
- Mistrust of leaders, churches and faith organisations
- The lasting blatant, but sometimes subtle deposits of trauma that seep into many spheres of life

In essence it is surviving, remaining, persisting and enduring in faith when individuals come to the realisation of what has happened to them.

In the cold light of day when the cards are laid on the table and we see people, experiences and encounters for what they really are, it is that which we need to survive. It is surviving faith in humanity, faith in God and even faith in ourselves. Faith in ourselves to make the right decisions, after all there were sometimes choices we may have made that led us into certain places and certain relationships. In no way is that to "victim blame" but from personal experience I have asked myself many questions about, 'why I stayed at Eden House for so long?' and 'why I didn't make different life decisions etc.?' This can often lead us to doubt our ability to manage our lives well, and it's very easy to continue in submissive environments, reverting back to old patterns. We will explore more as we walk through the chapters of my story and others detailed in the pages of this book. I hope you can now see why this book is 'surviving' spiritual abuse.

Is Spiritual Abuse In The Bible?

That's a great question. The phrase 'spiritual abuse' is not found in the Bible, however I would argue that there are incidents and themes that demonstrate the fallen nature of mankind to engage and illicit in the types of behaviour, actions and words that constitute spiritual abuse.

As Spirit filled, born again, Jesus-loving Christians, the Bible is our standard, example and pattern for living, not the world, the government, culture or society. As such it is the Bible that ought to remain our standard and the tool with which we measure ourselves against. We ought to desire to live and lead in an exemplary manner.

The Bible states:

> *Beware of false prophets, who come to you in sheep's clothing, but inwardly they are ravenous wolves. You will know them by their fruits. Do men gather grapes from thornbushes or figs from thistles?*

Matthew 7:15-16 NKJV

The picture of a wolf in sheep's clothing demonstrates a sly, deceptive and deadly intent. To masquerade, pretend and therefore infiltrate the sheep unnoticed is wicked, but such is the nature of a ravenous wolf. They are in fact hungry and pre-dispositioned to desire the destruction that leads to death. It is their inherent nature that drives them to behave in this manner. The construct of a wolf in sheep's clothing represents 'false prophets'. A prophet is the mouthpiece of heaven, an oracle, who unveils the mysteries of God. They bring good news, judgement and revelation, but at heavens command and for a set purpose. However, to be a false prophet is to be fake, a poorly constructed copycat version that originates from a different source. The Bible says we are to beware, to take notice of and be careful of these people, which have ungodly inner motivations rather than healthy, wholesome and righteous intentions. It could be argued, that these 'wolves in sheep's clothing' are the very creatures that control, manipulate and spiritually abuse the sheep, or the people, in their congregations.

In the book of Ezekiel we see that there were wicked leaders in the house of Israel,

> *The conspiracy of her prophets in her midst is like a roaring lion tearing the prey; they have devoured people; they have taken treasure and precious things; they have made many widows in her midst.*
>
> Ezekiel 22:25 KJV

This again is an example of the destruction that leaders or prophets can have on the people.

> *Beloved, do not believe every spirit, but test the spirits, whether they are of God; because many false prophets have gone out into the world. By this you know the Spirit of God: Every spirit that confesses that Jesus Christ has come in the flesh is of God*
>
> 1 John 4:1-2 NKJV

You may be asking "What about those leaders who confess Christ, but still act incorrectly and inappropriately?" Romans 11:29 teaches us that:

> *... the gifts and the calling of God are irrevocable.*

As such, we cannot only focus on the gifts of a person, it is imperative we also take note of the fruit they produce.

Psalm 23, is a familiar Bible passage that exemplifies the role of a shepherd or a leader through which we can learn several aspects with relation to the standard, characteristics and behaviours of a good leader.

> 1. *The Lord is my shepherd; I shall not [a]want.*
>
> 2. *He makes me to lie down in [b]green pastures; He leads me beside the [c]still waters*
>
> 3. *He restores my soul; He leads me in the paths of righteousness For His name's sake.*
>
> 4. *Yea, though I walk through the valley of the shadow of death, I will fear no evil; For You are with me; Your rod and Your staff, they comfort me.*
>
> 5. *You prepare a table before me in the presence of my enemies; You anoint my head with oil; My cup runs over.*
>
> 6. *Surely goodness and mercy shall follow me All the days of my life; And I will dwell in the house of the Lord Forever.*
>
> Psalms 23:1-6 NKJV

Let's look a little more deeply at a couple of these verses and what we can learn about Godly leadership versus abusive or controlling leadership.

♦ **Verse 1 The Lord is my shepherd, I shall not want**

The primary role, function and purpose of a Shepherd is to take care of their sheep, to look after, nurture and raise them. It is a role of service and care taking that establishes a relationship between a sheep and their shepherd. As a result, the sheep does not want, or is not in a state of need, because there is the assurance and knowledge that the shepherd provides and makes plans for provision.

This is understood to mean that a good leader knows their role, and understands that without the people they serve they would not be able to lead. Their role is to provide reassurance and security that God is able to meet all the needs of the congregation, and they must play their part well.

A Godly leader takes care of and serves those they lead

A leader with abusive tendencies does not put the needs of people first and does not make the appropriate provision to ensure their needs are met in a healthy manner.

♦ **Verse 2 He makes me to lie down in green pastures; He leads me beside the still waters.**

A good shepherd allows time for sheep to rest. They not only allow them time, but they ensure that the space or environment in which they rest in is suitable. They lead the sheep to sustenance - grass to eat and still waters to drink from. I remember reading about the significance of still water; because a sheep's nose and mouth is quite close together they would find it very hard to drink in moving or choppy water as the water would go up their nose. I often picture the lengths a shepherd may have to go to, in order to find that still water. How many fast moving brooks of water would he walk by and how many streams, all in search of that 'still' water. This speaks of sacrifice in providing for the sheep.

This teaches us that a good leader does not force people to keep going. There used to be a Duracell advert about going on and on, but people aren't Duracell batteries, rest is needed.

A good leader supports and facilitates this. They serve their congregation and encourage them to rest and have time out. A good leader also ensures the right sustenance is found – healthy, appropriate, life giving nutrition mentally, emotionally and spiritually.

A Godly leader makes sacrifice and provision for those they serve

Therefore, a poor leader is found lacking in these areas and is more self-serving, than serving others.

+ **Verse 3. He restores my soul; He leads me in the paths of righteousness**

A shepherd restores, in other words, refreshes and rebuilds the life of their sheep. The fact that it's plural shows that it's not a one off thing. It's not just one time, maybe in response to an incident, but it's a continual and intentional way of taking care and looking after sheep.

A Godly leader is a bridge for healing and restoration and instructs in the way of righteous living.

Therefore, behaviour or words that destroy the soul, the mind and the emotions of an individual, will lead them down a path of destruction. This is what a controlling, manipulative and abusive leader may harbour.

In John 10:12 we learn:

> But a hireling, he who is not the shepherd, one who does not own the sheep, sees the wolf coming and leaves the sheep and flees; and he wolf catches the sheep and scatters them.
> John 10:12 NKJV

A hireling, someone who only works for reward is often self-seeking. They do not care about the welfare of those in their care. They abandon their posts and do not execute the necessary protection when an enemy or adversary approaches. Leaders of leaders who fail to ensure that those they have responsibility for are safeguarded and protected are tools of destruction.

A 'leader' who does not genuinely care for, and put the needs of those they lead first, are often at risk of harming them in some way. This can be the start of spiritual abuse, and unfortunately it is very common. Spiritual abuse does however manifest in very different ways for different people. When I started writing my own story for this book I was inspired to invite other survivors of spiritual abuse to share their stories. To give voice to their experiences and language to their struggle. Throughout the book you will meet several courageous individuals, and the first person I would like to introduce you to is Tina.

Tina D's Story

I never expected that one of the most traumatic experiences of my life would come through a leader in the church which I was a member of. It is something that shook me to my core as the incident was unexpected and seemed to come from nowhere.

Although it happened 12 years ago, I remember the day as if it was yesterday. I, along with six other church leaders were in a leadership meeting. I was taking the meeting minutes, as I supported with admin, finance and secretarial aspects of church life. We had nearly reached the end of the agenda and were on the subject of team building. Another leader had made a suggestion that it would be nice to go bowling, or do an activity together, so we can be open with one another. It's like that was the match that caused the volcano to erupt inside one of the Senior leaders, we'll call her 'Rose.' She started on a cynical rant about opening up ... 'you want people to open up, some people are as closed as a fish, but they know how to take your husband off to a hotel'

She started shouting loudly at me and insinuating I had something going on with her husband as we had gone off into a hotel together, and '... if I thought that was acceptable, then something was wrong, and if you have anything to say you should say it in front of me...' She went on and on, and it shook me to my core. She was very aggressive and stunned the whole meeting into silence, after which things went from bad to worse in her and her husband's Charles behaviour towards me and general attitude.

Just to be clear, I had gone for a church business meeting with Charles in a café, located in a hotel. It was a public place and there was no hidden agenda, and this was not uncommon as we had no designated church office. The fact of the matter was there had been other female church members who had 121 meetings with Charles, who was the Senior Leader, as part of general church life. Other leaders had remarked that they went for meetings, Rose was aware, and it was no issue. So it then became clear that I was being targeted, and there was a very uncomfortable atmosphere.

Rose would always watch me in church, sometimes leaving her seat and going to the back of the hall. I was not being paranoid, but I could feel her eyes on me and if I glanced around, her eyes would meet mine. It's as if I wasn't "allowed" to speak to her husband Charles, even though it was only ever about the church admin, secretarial and finance areas, as she would appear out of nowhere, sometimes snatching things out of my hand. It was awkward and uncomfortable.

On the day of the incident I left the leadership meeting stunned and shocked, it affected me so greatly that I even damaged my car driving. I felt like I was in a traumatized daze, still not quite believing that the humiliating experience had really just happened, as it was unbelievable. A few days later, I did receive a 'token' apology, but the issue was not addressed, and the tables were turned and I was accused of being rude and having an attitude.

It was soul destroying, I suspected that Rose had an issue with me, but had no idea how deep this was. I felt so bad, it would have been better to have been stabbed with a knife. It was so humiliating. I felt church should have been a safe, secure and supportive place, but it was the total opposite, and it was the beginning of me losing faith in human beings, and the ability to trust. It was a toxic environment.

Despite this, I stayed at the church, as I believed I was serving God and genuinely wanted to help, up until a few years ago when they made the decision to get rid of all the leaders. I was committed for almost 20 years in so many *areas of the church. I felt like I had been treated like rubbish. I spent the next year in a daze, hardly even wanting to go to church. At the moment I go to a large church and choose not to get involved because of what I have experienced. It's like I am unconsciously living in a self-protective stance. There were times I felt God failed me, and questioned why He allowed this to happen. In spite of it all I continue to trust God.*

Chapter Three

The Price For Sin

We Are All Human And Make Mistakes

*O*ften times I reflect on this part of my story in utter disbelief. I honestly feel like I have experienced every range of emotion over the years, not so much when the situation occurred, but more so when I realised exactly what had occurred. Let me set the scene …

There was a particular man at Eden House, who we'll call Howard. He was a committed and long standing member, he also served on the leadership team in different roles. I never took much notice of Howard, I mean he was there serving, but as a single woman at that time, I never took "notice" of him other than as another brother in Christ. He was also single, and there came a point when he expressed an interest in me. We began talking more and everything was going fine. I began to develop feelings for him, but not so much because I genuinely liked him, it was more that I liked that he liked me, and I appreciated the attention, in all honesty.

There were times it would be just he and I working in the church office, and I would sometimes drop Howard home. It was during these car journeys that there was a shift in how he would talk to me. He became more suggestive in his comments and sometimes touched my leg etc. I really didn't know how to react. On hindsight alarm bells should have been ringing at that point. Maybe it was his persistence, maybe it was my appreciation of the attention but we ended up meeting up on a few occasions after that and started getting more physical with each other. At the time my carnal thinking was "as long as you didn't have sex, everything up to that point was OK... after all we're human!!" Of course that was not acceptable, I had a friend share with me recently that for many believers, passion outweighs purity, unless purity becomes their passion. In that season of my life purity as my passion was more spoken about than actually lived out.

Anyhow, after a few weeks of fooling around, one evening things went much further than I had planned or wanted and we ended up being intimate. I was devastated. Literally I felt completely heartbroken. In the midst of my sin I was repentant, and full of regret. I loved Jesus, had committed to serving him, made a decision to save myself for marriage and here I was in my late 20's feeling I had messed up.

The following day as I was driving to work I remember feeling sick to my stomach as I recalled the events of the previous night. I made a brief detour and was on my way to speak with one of the women leaders at church, who I was particularly close to, so I could confess that I had slept with Howard.

I shared that I needed to step down from leading at Eden House where I was a trainee minister, because of my sinful mistake. My journal entry from that week detailed the grief and heartache, and also that I had been 'rebuked and corrected' by the leader. That leader told the Senior Pastor, and a meeting was called. I was distressed; devastated that in my view I had allowed this to happen and was so repentant before God. The depth of my sorrow was visible, basically I was an emotional wreck.

Later that week the day of the scheduled meeting with the Pastor had arrived. He had instructed both Howard and I to meet him at the church office. As a side note would you agree that there are some experiences that feel like they will be forever etched in your memory bank, possibly for a good reason, but most likely for a bad reason. In my case it was the latter. I sat in that meeting feeling ashamed and defeated. The Pastor looked at both of us and asked some very personal and intimate questions about exactly what had happened. I recall feeling so humiliated and wishing that I could just wake up from this nightmare. At one point the Pastor turned to Howard and said, "but we've been here before with you…" I was stunned into silence. I thought this man had been pursuing me because he was genuinely interested, only to find out that I was one of who knows how many women. I was also in shock to learn that the Senior leadership was aware of this man's proclivity, and in my view did not ensure it was addressed and the appropriate safeguards put in place. The whole meeting was painfully uncomfortable, and awkward. The pastor asked Howard to go, and then I was left alone with him.

We spoke about a few things, and it was then that the Pastor advised that in order to bring reconciliation between me and God and me and him I had to pay a sin offering. I had never heard of this before. A "sin offering." At the time I was so distressed at all that had happened I simply listened intently to what the pastor was saying to me. I trusted him and I was ready to obey. You see this was a Pastor I had known for many years, I considered him to be family. He was my Pastor, someone I looked up to and greatly respected. At that time there was nothing inside of me that questioned his instruction. There were a few others things advised including that I should spend time with the Pastor's family at their home to recover, and I did so as an 'obedient child of God'. In addition, it was advised that I go get checked out. I was living in a literal nightmare. I cannot even describe how heartbroken I was, that I found myself in this situation. After all, I grew up in the *'I kissed dating goodbye'* era, and although I was in no way perfect, I really had been trying to save myself for marriage. Unfortunately, I had succumbed to Howard's persuasive ways.

Before the meeting concluded the Pastor suggested the three figure amount that would suffice as an acceptable "sin offering." I was to bring the offering in the office and Pastor would receive it, pray for restoration after which reconciliation would happen. It all sounded so easy, like a formula. A + B = C! No one knew what had taken place in the office. Howard and I never discussed it. I do not know whether he was instructed to do the same. But off I went on my merry way, slightly relieved that we had a plan in place. It was a few days later that I returned to the office for another one-to-one meeting with the Pastor, as I now had my monetary "sin offering" to present. As he took it, I felt like some of the burden was being lifted and remember the touch of his cool, clammy hands as he held my hands within his and prayed for me.

The Pastor shared many things about what he felt I needed to do. This included taking some time out from ministry and how I should be praying. I felt I needed to do everything he said, after all he was Gods servant and surely faithfully obeying him would mean I would get back into Gods good books, which I so desperately, desperately wanted. It had been an emotional roller coaster. However, four weeks later, with no counselling, I was permitted to continue in my trainee minister roles. Life had outwardly returned to normal. I had done enough begging, crying and pleading with God to forgive me and the sin offering felt like the cherry on the top that secured my forgiveness and reconciliation >*sigh*< I was thankful and appreciative and thought nothing more of the situation.

On reflection, whilst I believe that restoration is needed when leaders make mistakes or fall into sin, I do believe that there should have been counsel and accountability to check one's readiness to serve. Or in fact if they should be serving at all. It is not entirely surprising, and in some ways understandable that no appropriate support was put in place, given that the solution for my sin was mismanaged. At Eden House it often felt that to be seen to be presenting a good ministry image was the most important thing. In fact, far more important and valuable than helping individuals work through their own personal struggles and inner conflicts. So life carried on and I was OK, or so it seemed. I was good at burying issues and just getting on with things, never realising that I was a walking time bomb of emotional fragility.

The year after the 'sin offering' incident I left Eden House, and I will share more about that in a later chapter. Shortly before I left a friend from work had invited me to visit an independent Bible study group with her. I continued to attend Bible Study regularly and it was an environment I felt safe in and one in which I was learning, as well as receiving ministry, counsel and support. Attending this group became increasingly important after I left Eden House. The following year, after leaving Eden House, the Bible study leader began a study on righteousness. This would be the mechanism to begin the unveiling of a cloud of deception that I had been unconsciously living in for a long time.

We had been on the topic of righteousness for several weeks, as we were reading a Derek Prince book called *Atonement*. I had found it fascinating and uplifting to be fed with Biblical truths, in a profoundly different and enriching way. But I will never forget the day that same truth in some way felt like it destroyed what I had previously believed was truth.

Someone was reading a portion of the book explaining that Jesus' sacrifice on the Cross meant that all the old testament sacrifices were no longer necessary. They began to read through some of them; the grain offering and the wave offering and then yes, there in black and white the 'sin offering' was also listed. I felt like a ton of bricks had hit me. Whilst they continued reading and discussing the next part of the chapter, I felt stuck. Stuck on the amazing revelation that Jesus' sacrifice meant that none of the old testament offerings for sin were no longer necessary. Stuck on what that now meant for me. Stuck on the painful truth that I had to recall that the Pastor whom I looked up to, respected and believed had deceived me. Stuck that I had been lied to and I now needed to process a completely different take on a hugely significant event from my past. Whilst we know that the truth will set us free, the journey to freedom may not be a smooth and painless ride!

As I was stuck and reeling from not knowing what to think

next, I arranged a one-to-one meeting with my Bible Study Teacher and began sharing parts of my personal journey. She became a confidant; she is a wise mature woman of God who was sent into my life at a time I needed her. I felt comfortable enough to share what had taken place leading up to the 'sin offering' incident and the finances that had been requested. I recall her response was one of absolute shock as she remarked

"A what?" … "A … a sin offering," I hesitantly replied.

We went back to scripture, after which I knew without a shadow of a doubt, that what had happened was wrong, manipulative and deceptive. At that time, I was not aware of the term spiritual abuse, but that in essence is what it was. Inappropriate and emotional manipulation of God's word for financial gain.

Let's take a look together at exactly what the Bible says. Leviticus Chapter 4, speaks about the sin offering, and details, specific instructions in which the Priests were meant to follow, to make atonement for the sin committed. The 'sin offering' was a mechanism in which an unblemished goat or lamb, was sacrificed. The sin of the person was transferred to the animal, who was then slaughtered, to pay the price for the sin, and restore order. All the sin offerings and sacrifices in the Old Testament were a shadow or type of what Christ would fulfil in the New Testament through His sacrifice on the Cross.

In the book of Hebrews in the New Testament it says:

> 1.For the law, having a shadow of the good things to come, and not the very image of the things, can never with these same sacrifices, which they offer continually year by year, make those who approach perfect. 2 For then would they not have ceased to be offered? For the worshippers, once purified, would have had no more consciousness of sins. 3 But in those sacrifices there is a reminder of sins every year. 4 For it is not possible that the blood of bulls and goats could take away sins. 5 Therefore, when He came into the world, He said: "Sacrifice and offering You did not desire, But a body You have prepared for Me. 6 In burnt offerings and sacrifices for sin You had no pleasure. 7 Then I said, 'Behold, I have come— In the volume of the book it is written of Me—To do Your will, O God.' " 8 Previously saying, "Sacrifice and offering, burnt offerings, and offerings for sin You did not desire, nor had pleasure in them" (which are offered according to the law), 9 then He said, "Behold, I have come to do Your will, O God." He takes away the first that He may establish the second. 10 By that will we have been sanctified through the offering of the body of Jesus Christ once for all. 11 And every priest stands ministering daily and offering repeatedly the same sacrifices, which can never take away sins. 12 But this Man, after He had offered one sacrifice for sins forever, sat down at the right hand of God'
>
> Hebrews 10:1-12 NKJV

The truth is that for the born again believer, through the finished work of the Cross and the Resurrection of Jesus we have been made righteous and our sins have been forgiven. Don't get it twisted when we make mistakes we must repent and ask God for forgiveness.

The Word teaches us:

> *If we say that we have fellowship with Him, and walk in darkness, we lie and do not practice the truth. But if we walk in the light as He is in the light, we have fellowship with one another, and the blood of Jesus Christ His Son cleanses us from all sin. If we say that we have no sin, we deceive ourselves, and the truth is not in us. If we confess our sins, He is faithful and just to forgive us our sins and to cleanse us from all unrighteousness*
>
> 1 John 1:6-9 NKJV

It is clear that it's the blood of Jesus that cleanses us from sin, because He paid the price. One of the first prayers that many of us learn as children is the Lord's prayer found in Matthew chapter 6. It reads:

> *Our Father in heaven, Hallowed be Your name. Your kingdom come. Your will be done On earth as it is in heaven. Give us this day our daily bread. And forgive us our debts, As we forgive our debtors. And do not lead us into temptation, But deliver us from the evil one. For Yours is the kingdom and the power and the glory forever. Amen. "For if you forgive men their trespasses, your heavenly Father will also forgive you. But if you do not forgive men their trespasses, neither will your Father forgive your trespasses.*
>
> Matthew 6:9-15 NKJV

It is evident that we "confess" our sin or in other words willingly admit to the wrong and verbally acknowledge it to God who will then be true to His nature and His word. He will both forgive and cleanse us from everything unrighteous. The one condition that Jesus spoke about in regards to being forgiven was forgiving others.

The Scriptures above teach us that for us who live after

the resurrection, the method through which we receive forgiveness is not through paying a monetary sin offering, rather accepting that Christ already paid the ultimate price and we appropriate that today through confessing our sins, asking for forgiveness, having made sure we have forgiven others.

That which had occurred to me was a heart wrenching and painful truth to be realised. I had numerous upsetting thoughts about the fact that I was told I had to financially pay to be reconciled to God. When in fact the finished work of the Cross; the death, burial, resurrection and ascension of Christ was perfectly complete. This was tough.

I was tormented with the thought that I had been used when I was at my most vulnerable for financial gain. Tormented for many years wandering who else may have known. Yet I also knew I had to go on a journey of forgiveness and healing.

It is said that hindsight allows us to see in 20:20 vision and I used to wonder why I didn't question what the Pastor said, or even read up on it myself, but I didn't. This was partly due to the fact that I was so distressed about the whole situation that I was willing to cling onto anything that would alleviate my emotional distress. In addition, I believe I did not question the notion of a 'sin offering' because I was deeply embroiled in the type of church culture wherein we were so used to being 'fed.' Fed from the Word several times a week, so much so that there was never a thought that I needed to study and learn things for myself. Strange, but true.

Even as I write, I have several thoughts going through my mind, about sharing on this level, but the most domineering thought is the reminder of why I write. I write to you and I have chosen to expose personal details of my journey, my weaknesses, my failings and my mistakes. This is for the sole purpose of allowing God to bring healing, hope and deliverance to those of you who are broken, frustrated and hurt, because you can, in some way relate to the stories in this book.

CHAPTER FOUR

Could There Be More Painful Truths?

How Could I Not Have Known?

*C*an I share a behind-the-scenes moment in the life of an author? Of all the aspects of what I went through this was the one I had struggled with the most, in deciding whether to include it in the book or not. If you are reading this chapter, I guess it made the final edit because I knew deep down that my truth will be freedom for some of you. I am sure there may be differing opinions on this part of my journey and that's OK. Something I love to share with clients I coach and mentor is that everyone will always have an opinion on you, your life and your decisions. If we constantly bend to them (never mind the fact that they change their opinions as often as they change their socks), we may never fulfil the very purpose for which God sent us onto the earth for! So here I am paying less attention to what some may think and focussing on the journey to freedom.

As a caveat there is light at the end of the tunnel, and remember this book is a story of hope and restoration and I share my truth from a very healed place. So if you're ready, let's continue.

As I mentioned previously, I left Eden House about a year after the 'sin offering' incident and a couple years after that I kept having a really disturbing and recurring dream. I kept dreaming that I was being raped, violently. I was being raped by two men. It was graphic, I mean really graphic and I found it distressingly disturbing. There could be many ways of interpreting this dream, it is always important to be discerning as to what a dream may mean and also the appropriate response. I prayed about them, rebuked the dreams and yet they continued.

Whilst I was settled in a new church by then, I still had my guard up during this time, and chose to go for counsel with my Bible study teacher. It took a lot of courage, because it's not exactly a regular type of thing that you share. 'Oh yeah last week I went to the shops, ran some errands, bumped into an old friend and also dreamt about being raped!' Nowhere near normal … even to say the 'r' word was near impossible.

So I sat down in the comfortable chair that I was very used to, we make small talk and then my Bible Study Teacher asked, "How is everything?" in that manner that indicated it was now time to share what was really on my mind. I took a deep breath, decided it was now or never and feeling slightly self-conscious shared the dreams that I had been having. At one point I felt like this shouldn't be me. This shouldn't be me sitting here. This shouldn't be me having this discussion because this really shouldn't be happening to me.

Irrespective of and despite the shouldn't, couldn't, wouldn't this was my present reality.

So my Bible study teacher listened and in a calm, ever so gentle manner asked, "Has this ever happened?" I quickly replied no. I mean how could it have, of course there was the sleeping with Howard thing, but that's been dealt with. I am a grown woman, I remember thinking to myself, *if something like that had happened to me of course I would know.*

However, over the next few days I felt the Holy Spirit ever so gently take me back in my mind to the night that I had slept with Howard and walk me through exactly what had really happened. It was like looking back in clear daylight, entirely sober and through squeaky clean lenses.

During that evening I had told him to stop, I had told him no, I had asked him to stop, to please stop ... and he didn't. In fact, he had told me to wait. He was physically stronger than me. I felt sick to my stomach. I was in utter shock that I found myself in a situation that I did not want to be in.

In hindsight it's so easy to condemn myself about why I didn't push him off. Why didn't I fight him off? Why didn't I just do something? It was not what I wanted. The incessant questions I asked myself and the desire to change the past, could not actually change anything. That night, I felt powerless, scared and fearful.

If you understand something about the physiological human response to fear, there are often three main reactions; fight, flight or freeze. It's not a conscious, processed decision, it's an unconscious automatic survival response that occurs in one of those three ways. If I could have chosen differently, I would have, but I didn't - I froze.

In my frozen state I disengaged mentally, emotionally and physically. I was in utter disbelief, shock, and all I felt was the shame and guilt that I was in this situation. The deceptive and overarching thought was that I had chosen this. I was so utterly consumed with the shame, guilt, condemnation ...

then more shame and guilt. To the point that that I had never been able to see the situation for what it really was until that time. Three years later.

Unconsented sexual intercourse. Rape.

The pain, the anguish was once again devastating, as I began to process this new truth to what was already a painful situation. I was confused that this could have happened to me and I didn't even realise! Maybe because the 'r' word which was how I thought about it in the first few years after learning the truth had always conjured up images of dark valleys, violence and being held at gun point by a strange man. However, statistics indicate that sexual assault including rape, inappropriate touch, unwanted attention and advances of a sexual nature are often carried out by someone known personally to the victim (although I prefer to use the term survivor).

There is also the issue of 'victim blaming' and the common narrative that the survivor must have led the perpetrator on, or is crying wolf. I truly believe this is a tragedy that keeps many trapped in a prison of silence. They often feel scared to speak out, because they think they won't be believed. I'll introduce you to Olivia shortly. Olivia is one survivor who was not believed and this forms part of her story. After all, when it comes to sexual assault in a church community the ramifications are many. The manipulation and control becomes perpetuated when the perpetrator is able to keep just enough people on side. Just enough people seeing their 'good, righteous and holy' masquerade. So much so that their character would stand up to close scrutiny in the event that an accusation was ever made.

It's important to recognise that deception is multi layered

and complex. It is also a spiritual force and when you are in a controlling and spiritually abusive environment, it can compromise your ability to recognise truth, and make courageous choices. These situations and incidents are complex and painful, but I must reiterate there is healing after tragedy. There is restoration after brokenness. Like so many others, I am a living testimony of what Jesus can do. I forgave Howard, and felt free.

Incidentally the recurring dreams of me being raped ceased.

I honestly felt like I spent years with tears in my eyes, constantly waiting to roll down my face. I was crying over what I had been through, and often this was in the presence of God. My beautiful, now late, Granny had once taught me that whenever I feel pain because of a heartache, turn that cry into worship, and the pain will be relieved. Let me tell you, it works. It certainly wasn't a one-time thing, but worshipping definitely helped and was an integral part of my healing process over the years.

Pain is interesting and can easily be camouflaged, because if you saw me outside of my home during that time, you would never have known what I was going through. How many of us muster the strength to keep holding it together? Putting on a brave face, day after day after day. Pushing the pain down, as if pushing the pain away, all whilst supporting, encouraging and helping others. We are so good at reminding others to take care of themselves, advising them to get the help and support they need. All the while ignoring the fact that we need to do the same for ourselves.

As people, we can often walk around with painful secrets, shrouded in a deceptive cloak of shame, whilst still thinking we must be to blame. The fear about not being believed. The concern that it was so many years ago, so it really shouldn't matter anymore. The confusion that 'it' or 'they' weren't all bad, because we may still have a strong sense of loyalty and attachment, so is it really the right thing to do to rake it all up again?

Even in the natural, if a wound is not exposed how can it be attended to and fully healed. Healing comes in different ways and many forms. But it begins when we are willing and brave enough to acknowledge that we do need the healing. Healing does not always mean confronting the individual, or demanding an apology, but it is does mean speaking to someone you feel safe with, maybe a counsellor, maybe a confidant and starting or continuing the journey of talking and praying through the situation.

But for now I speak to you, the individual, who is reading this chapter with tears in your heart, maybe filling your eyes, or streaming down your face. Maybe there is an ache in your chest and a pain in your gut. Beloved, Gods sees and God knows. Do not fear that digging up the past will be so painful that it will cause you to break. It is time. It is your time, healing awaits.

For those who may shed silent tears of compassion and sadness at my story, may your tears be transformed into prayers of intercession for the many who are not yet healed. Not yet healed from the wounds these types of situations inflict ... pray for them as if they were your child, your family member, colleague or church brethren. For they very well may be.

There are many lost souls, who have not only left church, but also left their faith because of hurt. Pray for them.

There are seniors walking around wounded. Walking around with taped up hurts; weeping in silence over the hurt and pain inflicted 10, 20, 30 or maybe even 40+ years ago.

Healing is available and has no time stamp or expiry date.

Olivia G's Story

My experience was totally unexpected, and what followed was even worse I guess, I didn't expect the church to epically fail like it did. Nor the weird space I now occupy to be the norm, so normal that when lockdown happened, due to the global pandemic and everyone missed "church" I didn't. I didn't feel like I was missing anything. Although I usually attend church every week, and support other ministries on a Sunday, I am not necessarily in the same church every weekend, however this is not how it used to be.

There was a time when there was no way I would not attend Glinvale my old church on a Sunday. I would even leave my parents' house on a Saturday night or early Sunday morning and drive 2 hours to attend service at MY church. On the rare Sundays that I wasn't on the rota to do media, children's ministry or creative arts I served in which ever ministry team needed me. This meant that almost every Sunday I was serving. I had started the creative arts team in response to an earlier trauma in my life and headed the children's ministry team. I guess I have a ministry of helps, so if anyone needed me to get water, tea or stationery, I was the one to send or ask. Rain, snow or shine I was there, faithfully serving at Glinvale, so church became a major part of my life. I enjoyed it for a time but then it became where I was only giving out and serving, but not being filled back up.

It was just a regular Sunday where I was teaching the children, and as usual I was the first one in the church building and the last one out. I made sure I cleaned the children's area when we finished, as we the children's ministry had a bad reputation for giving the kids snacks and leaving a mess. By mess the church leaders meant the bins were full and the tables weren't always spotless, because we encouraged the children to tidy up after themselves. On this particular day the bins were full and overflowing and I went in search of a bin liner (having searched all the expected places – kitchen, cleaning cupboard, office cupboard, side room and store room etc.) as there was no sign of a bin liner anywhere. I spoke to the pastor I normally report to who sent me to the deacon, but I couldn't find him. A steward who was nearby offered to give me some assistance. He suggested I look in the basement, which no one ever wanted to go in alone, because the lighting was poor, stairs were rickety and it felt creepy. The steward offered to come with me and wait at the top of the stairs to make sure that I was okay. It was one of those rooms where you walk down dark stairs, as there was only one light in the middle of the basement. I walked down, had a look around and found the bin liners on a shelf. No sooner had I found them, I turned around and to my shock I found myself being kissed square on the lips with nowhere to escape. I stepped back into the shelving, with so many thoughts quickly flooding *my mind, as I had not seen or heard him following me. I exclaimed "oh" in place of a swear word to which he replied, "that was nice". Not really knowing how to respond I just said, "the kids will be waiting, I've got to go" and squeezed past him to leave the basement. I carried on with duties at church, too shocked to even process what happened. Later that day the steward contacted me with the suggestion of a "mutually beneficial" arrangement, in the sense that he wanted to meet for sex and in turn provide 'financial assistance" I guess he presumed that my position as a single student mother meant that this would be well received. I was offended and disrespected as I read the message, and also sad that a married man would make this 'offer'. I was left wondering how even in Glinvale, which is the house of God I could be so disrespected, left unguarded with no one to take care of my safety. I kept my distance every time I saw that steward at church, and on every occasion I fobbed him off, along with his 'offer' to spend time together whilst his family was away in return for what sounded like a stipend.*

I said nothing because Glinvale was one of those churches where everyone is either related or childhood friends or in a leadership position or godparents to someone…there were only a few of us 'outsiders' at this church. So, even if I complained, who would I complain to? What would I say and who would believe me?

Some months later, on what would again have been a normal Sunday at Glinvale, I was asked to minister in dance and I needed to quickly practice when I got to church.

No one else from the team was available, so I was going to do a solo piece. Although the service had started I needed the keys to access the appropriate rehearsal space. I couldn't find them in their usual place, so I approached one of the key holders who was a worship leader to ask for the keys to the key box. This was not unusual and I had been helped on occasions before. He offered to help find the keys in the very busy and disorganised key box. As we went down the corridor he walked up rather close behind me and I felt really uncomfortable, so I said "I'm gonna need you to back up" which was met with a laugh and half an apology, but he fell back in step. I carried on to the relevant office, without a second thought. When we got to the office we were both looking in the key box, comparing keys to find the right one. As I was holding different keys in both hands he turned and started kissing me and trying to undo my clothes. I was too stunned to move, as the last thing I expected, was to find myself being groped and being grabbed at whilst wearing my praise garments in the church office. I was frozen, after he kissed me he asked if I was okay. I asked him to stop and suggested that he should leave, I think I even said, I love your wife, she's my church sister, this is not an option. Then I asked if he was alright, he shook his head and said he was fine and left the office. I eventually found the key I needed, went back to the rehearsal space and carried on as though everything was normal. I was detached, disassociated and couldn't begin to even process what happened. I was also conscious that I was on the programme to minister and needed to serve in that way. I wasn't able to accept what happened and carried on attending church for 4 more months as though nothing had happened, it was like I was in a daze.

I didn't say a word to leadership, but carried on at Glinvale, as I had duties to fulfil. I was responsible for the children's ministry and could not just leave them, the team was already short staffed. I held children's services and rehearsals. I continued to dance and do other things and just 'tried' to move on. A few months later I attended a youth conference out of town and after that I just never went back to Glinvale. At first I blamed it on the travel dates as I was out of the country for 2 Sundays, then I said I was tired, then sick… then something else. There were endless reasons why I wasn't able to attend. Eventually my dance leader had worn me down with her consistent questioning as to what was going on, and I told her what had happened. She said I had to report both incidents as a duty of care to others who may be in the same position but without a voice, and that I needed to ensure the children and other vulnerable women would be protected. A month later at the end of 2018, I took another leader with me to meet with 2 pastors, one of which is the safeguarding officer regionally. I was comfortable with these three who I had confided in. It was not an ideal situation, but the leader who came with me, despite being related to one of the perpetrators always pushed me to address the matter. The pastors were close with the other leader and the other one was related to one of the other pastors. Everyone involved had a position. Everyone was related and connected in one way or the other.

I was told that the two situations, involving two different members of the church would be investigated and I was later asked for further information. I sent the relevant screenshots and details, was interviewed over the phone and left to wait for a response. Whilst the complaint was being investigated the worship leader took a sabbatical and the other steward continued in post. Several months later, I was called and told that the steward said it was a misunderstanding on my part and the worship leader had written a letter of apology. I was admonished, by the safeguarding pastor, not to put myself in positions where married men would assume I was extending an invitation and to let it go.

The next question was when would I be returning to church as my roles were waiting for me. No one checked on my wellbeing through the investigation process. About a month before I made the formal complaint I attended Glinvale for a memorial service as I was hosting a visiting dance team. The only pastor to ask where I had been and who I would have wanted to talk to was related to a perpetrator, so I felt I could not open up. It was very isolating and disempowering because I felt there was no one to turn to.

The secondary aftermath was worse; the senior pastor began to question me at every juncture he saw me. When I would be returning and saying he did not even know why I left, and remarking that I had just abandoned my post. Also that if I was avoiding a certain someone, they no longer *attended the church, (incidentally both parties still do and maintain their posts). I explained the situation and was asked if I needed deliverance as multiple people were doing this to me, maybe I was attracting it. I felt like I had been dropped, I was not in a safe space, I was not being heard. It was the moment I realised that I was not cared for and a spiritual daughter as I thought I was. I was told I needed to share the intimate details of what had allegedly happened as no one had informed him as the Bishop of the church, about the matter. However, I was aware of the structures in place to ensure he knew of every complaint filed at the church, confirming that he did in fact know about the complaint and the level of detail. The Bishop further questioned my suitability to lead children's ministry, as he stated that 'if I was unable to report an assault against myself how could I protect the children in my care?' Despite everything, I was still expected to return to my post. No matter how many times I said I was uncomfortable and needed to recover I kept being told of my duty and how the "alleged" matter had been resolved.*

The safeguarding pastor also kept asking what more I wanted besides the letter of apology as if I complained expecting a certain outcome. Had it not been for my dance leader pushing me to make a complaint I never would have said a word because I just thought they wouldn't do anything anyway. What I experienced felt a thousand times worse. I felt blamed, I felt shamed, diminished and dismissed. I felt gas lighted, that it was all in my imagination and no married man would be so crazy as to approach me.

> I remember thinking, if I would have just agreed to be a mistress then the fall out would have been less. I could have just had an affair and moved on with my life. I wished I had said nothing. The breakdown of my own marriage, a failed relationship and a previous assault in the church by another married man were all brought up in my interactions with the senior pastor. Issues I had trusted him with were used as reasons why my experiences couldn't be true or trusted. I was treated as if I wasn't "grateful" for all that Glinvale church and leadership had done for me. I tried to return again 7 months after my complaint, but felt so much grief in my spirit I was unable to consider returning permanently.
>
> Throughout this process, I continued to explore and visit other churches weekly, I went on to create the structure where I have a monthly fast. I have a church where I pay my tithes and I sit under their leadership while I recover. I also have engaged with a therapist to start the healing process. I am on no ministry teams but I continue to train in the creative arts as God leads.

There are so many who tragically experience some form of sexual abuse or assault in the church. It is not right, it is so wrong, but please remember that this does not represent who God is. His character or His nature. For many the healing will by multi-faceted, a healing of your soul and also a healing of your perspective … how you view, see and understand who Jesus is.

CHAPTER FIVE

The Downward Spiral

*S*piritual abuse is very complex and multi layered, it can occur so subtlety at first, that you do not see or recognise it. In fact, in some way it becomes "normalised." One of the most helpful ways I can explain this, is in terms of 'how to boil a frog' (please don't try this at home). This is a parable that is often used to explain change. You see frogs by nature have sensitive skins. If you were to take a frog and place it in a pan of hot or boiling water it would immediately jump out as it feels the heat. However, if you place a frog in a pan of cold water on a stove, and then gently turn the heat up, the frog acclimatises to the changes of temperature in its environment. Eventually becoming used to and comfortable with the ever increasing heat. Unfortunately, if left, the frog would eventually boil to death, without trying to escape. In a similar way, when people become used to an environment, they can unintentionally acclimatise to toxicity as the subtle changes ensue bit by bit.

In my case it was several years of being in a church culture that did not invite, but rather dissuade questions. There was no room for healthy debate, even for the purpose of learning and understanding. If the actions of the leadership were questionable a Scripture that was often used to silence the outspoken was:

> *Do not touch My anointed ones, And do My
> prophets no harm.*

Psalm 105:15 NKJV

It was never taught contextually, instead only used to verbally beat the saints into submission.

Another aspect of acclimatisation is that everyone else is seemingly going along with it. Whatever that 'it' is. I recall an incident where I was instructed, not asked, to falsify records. When I questioned whether this was the right thing to do, the leader who spoke to me reminded me that it was for the Lord. There was a strong implication that by not doing something I deemed inappropriate I was not serving the Lord. For leaders who you esteem and have in some ways been a help and support to you, there are often mixed and confusing feelings of loyalty when you are asked to do what you deem incorrect. Thus compounding the inner turmoil.

It can be easy when you are out of the situation and using hindsight to look back with a clear understanding and interpretation of what is right and what is wrong. However, when you are in the middle of it, it's often very difficult. There are unknowns and quiet underlying streaks of fear that creep in, if you dare to say no or object. It can feel like you are somehow going against the will of God.

When news reports and articles are published highlighting an incident where a church leader has asked their members to participate in acts, which are obviously bizarre to the rest of society, onlookers often do not understand the complex set of circumstances involved. It was widely reported in the media that a South African Pastor instructed his members to go outside and eat grass, in the same manner that cows do. Another Pastor had reportedly advised his brethren to drink Dettol (a disinfectant normally used for cleaning surfaces or when very diluted can be used on the skin). This was to 'protect' them from sickness, tragically several of the church members consequently died. Again, from the outside looking in, most people do not understand why these churches members participated in these activities.

At the time of writing this book we are still in the midst of the coronavirus covid-19 pandemic. I read a news articles of a pastor based in the UK who was allegedly selling 'coronavirus protection kits' to his church members for £91. These contained oil and red string, and he claimed that by purchasing and using them they would be protected. Exploiting peoples fear, anxiety and uncertainties for monetary gain or fame is ungodly and not in alignment with the teaching of Christ. We cannot "pay" for protection. As believers we know there are principles in Scripture relating to seed, tithes, offering and first fruits. It is not however, meant to be interpreted in this 'packaged' way.

We do not understand or know what goes on in the minds of such leaders. We do not know whether they are simply deceived, extortionists, brain washed or just wicked. As hard as it is, we have to accept that mankind has a proclivity for evil, some to a greater extent than others.

So why do some believers seem to blindly 'go along' with the obviously absurd instructions from their leaders or pastors?

◆ Brain Theory

I studied psychology for 'A' level and then went on to complete a BSc in Psychology at university. I recall studying neuropsychology, and in simple terms the effect of experiences and knowledge on not only behaviour but how the brain is developed. We learnt that neural pathways, much like a path through a field are strengthened and more pronounced through repetition and repeated experiences. This 'pathway' then becomes clearly defined and in some cases an automatic or default pattern.

You may be wondering if we are still on the topic of spiritual abuse, and if you would bear with me I will explain where this fits and why it could be an important consideration. For example, let's take the concepts of 'respecting elders' and 'obedience without question.' In some families, cultures and communities this is a normal construct that runs throughout. Therefore, if an individual has grown up with a strong message that we respect elders, obeying without question, (which in some instances is entirely appropriate, though not always), that individual has developed strongly, defined neurological pathways that denote that these concepts are the norm. Such could be the strength of that pathway that when a task is asked that may seem to them contradictory to an inner belief, the action and thoughts are set to the default position of 'respecting elders' and 'obedience without question', in other words 'do as you are told.'

This internal mechanism could be a hindrance for a victim or survivor of a spiritually abusive environment. This belief system may impede their ability to make the right choice when asked to engage in illegal, immoral, or unethical practices, as the argument of 'respecting elders' and 'obedience without question' proves strong and unwavering. This becomes the most dominant factor. To go against this way of being, would not only be seen as wrong, but in many instances would not even be a consideration. Feelings of powerlessness and predetermined defeat may prevail and as time goes on, as the incidents increase, the pathways only get stronger.

There is a common phrase that says 'you can't see what you are in, when you're in it, and only when you leave, can you really see it for what it really is.' It's funny how something can seem so unbelievable and obviously wrong when you are on the outside looking in. The experiences I encountered, all of which I have not detailed in this book, to safeguard others who were in some way connected to the church organisation, have put me in a position to in some small way understand why people stay in unhealthy, unwholesome and damaging relationships. Spiritual abuse can happen in relationships which has faith at its core, or other strong spiritual elements. Similarly, abuse can happen within other forms of relationships. The victim, or survivors' sense of distorted normality is one that has grown over a period time, and whilst judgement is clearly clouded, there is an underlying sense for them that 'this is the way it's meant to be.' This is normal.

• **The Role Fear Plays**

Fear. In the world of personal development and motivation, people often say **F.E.A.R.** is an acronym for:

False Evidence Appearing Real. Another popular alternative is Face Everything And Rise. Whilst these sound nice and appealing, the real fear that some survivors experience cannot be soothed or settled by either of these meanings.

Fear! Real, raw paralysing fear is suffocating and can cause one's stomach to become a knotted ball of anxiety. Fear does not always come about due to loud, threatening, outwardly and obvious aggression. It is often quiet, underlying ... almost as if it was not there, yet ever so present. At times the fear is induced by reminders of what happened to those who dared to disobey or leave the church. Often times it is matured and seasoned by a sense of needing to remain in an unhealthy place to be protected. The survivor then feels fear at the thought of leaving because of what might happen. They fear the negative repercussions not only from the organisation but potentially also from God. After all, these pastors and leaders were Gods representatives on earth, and their say was final. Seemingly respect is in order and the status quo is maintained. However, we know, that respect must be the mutual language of all concerned.

The Bible teaches that we are to fear and reverence God. Our fear of God therefore is the correct response to this instruction. The problem, is this command has been abused and misappropriated by some church leaders to keep the church in submission by demanding the same reverence and fear for themselves. We are called to honour, respect and obey our leaders in the Lord but not to be afraid or scared of them. (Obedience should be questioned when there is an obvious wrong, ungodly and unscriptural request or instruction being given). The Bible teaches:

> For God has not given us a spirit of fear, but of power love and a sound mind.
>
> 2 Timothy 1:7 NKJV

It also goes on to say that the perfect love of God casts out fear. (1 John 4:18) It is fair to argue that if someone is fearful of their pastor or leader this is unscriptural and may be a sign of spiritual abuse.

Behind all these factors is the demonic inspiration of the enemy. There are often spirits that operate on and through many that are spiritually abusive. Whilst we can provide some natural explanations for what happens, the whys and wherefores, behind it all is a satanic agenda, in which some leaders and organisations provide legs, arms and a voice through which this can be realised. Maybe not in every case, but in many.

Laura P's Story

The first incident I remember was back in 2003 from my then pastor. I went to him for help as I was experiencing difficulties in my marriage with my husband and I needed pastoral support and care. I believed that my Pastor would provide me with the support I needed, so I arranged with my husband to see our Pastor after church on a Sunday evening. I went to the meeting looking for that pastoral care, but experienced something very different. We started the discussions, and part way through he became very short and rudely stated "it had come to his attention that I was out nearly every night and I should be at home and be a good wife" His approach was very aggressive and I sat there absolutely shocked and demoralized. I felt humiliated in front of my husband and very unsupported. This pastor who at times was so lovely had now turned on me, it was almost like they were a Jekyll and Hyde character.

I went to the Pastor for help, but instead I left broken as he had beaten me down with his words. I then found out during the conversation that my husband had not only told the Pastor but also my house group leaders that I was never home. This was a lie. So not only was I dealing with the abuse from my pastor, but now also my husband was lying about me. I did go out to Prayer meeting on a Thursday and a Bible study with some friends on a Friday, but I was at home every other night of the week.

There was a lot going on and the ill treatment from my pastor added to the pressure.

This group of Friends who I had Bible study with kept me sane during this period of time, because I felt alone, abandoned and violated. I would pray and ask God what is going on. Each time I'd gone to see my pastor he would say the same thing over and over about me being an irresponsible wife who was never home. I would disagree with him and say I wasn't out all the time I take good care of my family. I would take my sons to church with me every Sunday, cook, clean and lovingly support my husband and children.

I was so broken I cried out to God asking Him please, please help me! Things were getting desperate at home. However, during that time as I was praying God did speak to me, and over the coming year things at home and in my marriage slowly improved. It hurt me deeply that my church and house group leaders did not support and help my family during that time and I never did trust them afterwards. I still attended church every Sunday though and served God.

There was another incident with the same pastor a few years later. I had asked to speak to him after the service on Sunday, as after praying and seeking God He had shown me that it was time to leave the church. I met with the Pastor in the foyer of the church and told him that I would be leaving. He went ballistic at me and began spewing negativity and stated "that my family would never amount to anything" I felt so betrayed.

The spiritual abuse incidents over the years have not only damaged me, but also my two children, who were verbally attacked by the youth leaders. They targeted my children, and blamed one stating he was the culprit following a situation. Our family was not liked and we felt it. The tragedy of these experiences is that although I tried to make things safe for my children, especially after we left they said they would never set foot in a church again because it was full of hypocrites. Heartbreaking.

A couple of months after leaving that church I started going to a new church and the Pastor was another male. However, he was very different, full of love and acceptance. I shared with him what had happened to me at my previous church and with the love of Jesus he really helped to restore me and my trust in a pastor again. This Pastor was so different he was loving, kind and understanding, it was just like being with Jesus. He explained that none of this was my fault and I was not responsible for the other Pastors actions towards me. This completely freed me and God restored me from a broken vessel to one that could be used for this glory. I was healing and on a journey of restoration.

Church life was going well and I was now in a leadership role and assisted in several areas. We had a new leader join our fellowship several years later. We welcomed them with open arms and at first they were great to work with. However, as time went on they would become very easily dissatisfied with the team and would say things to me like 'you are always dropping the ball'. They did not just say this once, but several times and it really put me on edge. They always wanted things done their way and if it was not done, this was made known. Additionally, they would always pick faults in what I did. It wasn't just me, they treated the other leaders the same way. One such instance happened when it was time for the minutes of last year's meeting to be printed off; these minutes could not be found on email or computer. I was the one who normally typed them up and saved them.

However, I did not do that this time around, it was another leader, who had lost the minutes. Sunday morning came and the individual was so angry they came at me like a roaring lion demanding to know where the minutes were. I said I do not know as I did not type them last time. They did not care, but instructed me to type them up again. I felt like I was being treated like a child. It was emotional and psychological abuse – I could not stop crying and it caused me to have stress and anxiety. I did type the minutes up ready for members meeting that evening. It was awful and I was so upset and stressed out that I had to take 3 days off work to recover from this awful experience.

This person would continue to treat me in a manner that was disrespectful until one day after going to my therapist about this instance I was challenged by my therapist to speak up and say to this person what they had done and how they made me feel. I said yes when I get a chance I will do so, but I was scared, however something needed to be done and said as it made me feel like I was never good enough. I had no peace of mind.

We had a leader's day and there was underlying tension. You could sense there was a white elephant in the room. At the end of the day, the person said does anyone have anything to add or say. I was fearful and petrified about speaking up, but the Lord had instructed me on what was going to happen. I found the courage to speak up and say yes I had something to say. I shared with the leader 'that it feels that whatever I do for you is never good enough and it has made me feel undervalued as a leader and minute taker.' I said that 'how I had been treated caused me stress and anxiety'. I didn't speak up to show that person up but I had to say how I had been treated had made me feel. It was like the flood gates were opened as my courage to speak invited others to also speak up and share. There were others who had even left the church because of this one leaders actions. The meeting cleared up the situation for me. The leader said they did not realise how they made others feel *and in time they started to change. I forgave them for all that happened. Several years later, I am still working with this leader, however I have my boundaries in place and no longer accept any mistreatment.*

CHAPTER SIX

Show Me The Door

And Then Everything Changed

*A*re there some days that have happened in your life that you can confidently say that you will never ever, EVER forget? They stand out as a day in which everything changed, a day that possibly started quite normal and routine, but ended vastly differently.

Mine happened on an uneventful Saturday in early winter. The day started really smoothly. I was still attending Eden House, but rather than go to the usual evening service, I had 'escaped' to fulfil a volunteering role at a Christian youth ministry. They were running a men's conference. I was part of the hospitality team and as we had completed all the necessary tasks we could sit down and participate in the service. I don't recall the specifics of what the minister was preaching, but I knew, in the core of my being, it made sense. I knew it was speaking to me. The message impacted me, it was a profound moment. At last I was hearing just the words I needed to hear. Words that I didn't even know I needed to hear. Has that ever happened to you?

I was so moved that when the minister gave an altar call to invite people forward for prayer if they wanted it, I stood up and went forward. I didn't have time to process that firstly

I was on team, and technically if we felt we needed prayer, we should wait till the end. Secondly that this was a men's conference, and here I was a young woman responding to the altar call! The reasons that would, or should have caused me to hold back in that moment became non-existent, as I made my way to the front.

The minister prayed for me and I remember him declaring "This is your time!" He prayed several things that are recorded in heaven, after which he went on to pray for the next person. As I was resting in God's presence at the altar I clearly heard, "IT IS TIME TO GO!" It was so loud, and came with a deep authority that although it is hard to fully put into words within the limited constraints of the English language, I knew, that I knew, that I knew it was God Himself who spoke those words to me. That is one fact that I can never deny. He had instructed me and I knew exactly that He had told me it was time to go. Time to leave Eden House. The rest of the day faded into a haze, but that moment remains crystal clear.

The following day was Sunday and I found myself getting ready for church, as although I knew what the Lord had spoken, I was still fearful to make the decision not to attend Eden House. Now for some of you reading this that is not really going to make much sense. But for those who have been in toxic atmospheres you will understand how "rules" are implied so strongly and severely that they are embedded and etched into your memory bank. I was scared as an adult to make my own decision about what to do.

I was "reminding" the Lord that I can't really just not go to church because I was meant to open the service, along with other responsibilities. Then all of a sudden I felt the

Lord stop me in my tracks. I heard and saw the word in my mind "REBELLION" ... "R-E-B-E-L" "L-I-O-N." I was deeply convicted in that moment that if I failed to heed what the LORD had spoken the evening before I would be in rebellion. Not just in rebellion, but I would be rebelling against the Lion of the tribe of Judah, one of the descriptions of Jesus. The instruction was clear and I chose to obey. Still uncertain and still apprehensive I called a leader from Eden House and I told them I wasn't coming to church, something I had never done before without having had an exceptional reason. The response from them was shock and disappointment, not stated, but I knew that tone in their voice. I ended the call with a sigh of relief, still unsure of what the coming days and weeks looked like, however for now I knew I had to obey. Church was so routine for me, I felt so lost that morning. I then remembered a dream I had earlier that week:

> I was stood in the front room of my house and I could see that the front door was wide open. I was putting on my shoes, and outside on the pavement, I recognised the senior pastors and the youth pastor from a local church. It is as if they had paused outside my house in order to wait for me to join them. They were dressed as if they were going on an outdoor hike – raincoats, rucksacks and walking boots.

Whilst I did not fully understand the dream, I thought there was no harm in me visiting that local church where they attended as a friend from work, was also a member there. So worst case scenario at least I'd see her for a catch up. It's the strangest thing how alien it felt attending a different church and not being in my normal environment, routine and responsibilities. I felt a little nervous going in, but was kindly ushered to a seat on the right side of the large 400 seater auditorium.

I enjoyed the service, although it felt really surreal thinking about the events that had happened the night before and what I knew the Lord had spoken to me. I could not tell you all the details of what the minister preached, but at one point he moved to the side of the auditorium where I was sitting and boldly declared, "some of you here need to come out from under a controlling spirit!" In that moment it was as if there was a spotlight shining right on me, and I knew, once again, without a shadow of doubt those words were meant for me. It was like the next piece of the puzzle in understanding the reality of a life I couldn't fully comprehend.

Some weeks went by and there happened to be a series of events that meant I could not attend Eden House. I was speaking at an event in hospital one weekend, travelled to see my family another weekend and so forth. It struck me during this time that no one had ever told me how to leave church, and what the protocol is. I mean when you leave a job you write a letter of resignation. When you move home you give notice and hand keys back. In recreational settings you cancel your membership, but no one had ever advised on how you should leave church.

Ironically there were always messages preached at Eden House, sometimes covertly, on the "importance" of staying where you've been planted, and that as leaders it's not healthy or right to be visiting other churches ... after all there was no other church in the city that was as anointed and on which the favour of God, miracles, signs and wonders rained down!! At the time I never questioned it too deeply, maybe because I had been conditioned to believe it. However, on reflection and in the clear light of day, some of the statements spoke of elitism and a self-exaltation that does not align with kingdom thinking.

I sat down and decided to write a letter of resignation, because I wanted to formalise, that I was stepping down from my areas of service. At the time of leaving I was a trainee minister and a youth leader. I also supported with the finance and some aspects of administration and was generally considered one of the 'pillars' of the church. In my naiveté I thought I would leave church, but would maintain the personal family like relationships I had not only with the pastor's family but the many other families I had become so close to over the years. I saw them more often that I saw my own family, often, willingly sacrificing important family occasions to "serve" at church.

The letter was not received or taken well, and so resulted in one of the most devastating conversation I have been unfortunate enough to be part of.

I was called into a meeting with the pastor at Eden House. Now this is someone I had known for many years and even considered family. I had travelled with them, stayed with them, been supported by them, and so yes, it was a meeting with my pastor; but more than that, he was an important and influential figure in my life. He was someone who I had looked up to and respected. So when he said I didn't hear from God, and that God wouldn't tell me to leave church,

I was confused. I felt like I was in a quandary … I knew I heard from God, but I was not being believed. Painfully the conversation was made more about them as I was told amongst many other things that, "At my age where am I going to find another Fran" … "If you leave, who is ever going to give you an opportunity to preach again?!" … "but you know me … some other men would have had you staying at their house and taken advantage of you …" I was so stunned.

I thought to myself; was I a commodity, that you would wonder where you would find another one of me?!

I was so broken that I accepted the statement about not speaking again, as at the time I had no emotional energy to fight it. And was I meant to be grateful … even thankful that you treated me right. Can I be really honest and say that even as a child of God who really loves Jesus there are times that expletives run through my mind, when I really sit back and reflect on what I had been told. Thoughts such as 'How dare you! … who do you think you are?' etc etc.

After several meetings and conversations that had ensued and after some months all the personal relationships I had formed at Eden House were lost. One of the biggest issues was, that the majority of my life at the time had been wrapped up in that church.

I felt lost. Alone. Broken

Can I pause and reflect for a minute on the goodness of God? During the year after the Lord started to bring new, solid, and wholesome people in my life and strengthen these relationships.

However, it was a still a heart achingly painful time. I remember after leaving the church being home for a few months. Wondering if I was even still a Christian as I was not going to church. Such had been the social conditioning and culture of Eden House. I thought my life was a hot mess. I literally felt like I did not know what life should look like, who was I without these roles, these titles, these connections and this association with Eden House.

During this time someone close to me would come to my house once a week so we could pray together and I spent so much time crying, devastated at such a big loss. But their support, love and prayers were invaluable, as they understood more of the situation than most.

Often times people may say 'how come you didn't tell people what was going?' But the truth of the matter is that most of us never knew ourselves what was really going on. At the time would I have said I was experiencing spiritual abuse? No. Partly because I had no idea that certain things were wrong and I had never even heard of the term spiritual abuse.

The end of my journey at that church was the beginning of a new chapter. As much as I would have wanted it to be all rose petals and butterflies, that was not the case. Far from it. It was the end of a painful chapter, and the beginning of a painful journey that would last years but eventually lead to healing, redemption and restoration.

One thing I have come to realise is that my experiences are not isolated and there are many similar accounts in other spiritual survivors' stories. The following is written by Henry, who recounts his own experiences of spiritual abuse:

Henry D's Story

I joined my former church in 2007, a year after I became a born again Christian. The church was smaller than the very first church I attended, and I thought that here I could grow spiritually. Everything started well; there were a few other young people, and I invited a lot of my friends to join me at the church. It was vibrant, multi-cultural; I myself am Congolese and everyone got along fine. In 2012 I was ordained as a youth pastor, and that's when the first alarming thing happened to me personally. The week after I got ordained there was a leadership meeting with the Pastor, elders and new leaders. There were about 6 of us in total. The pastor said; "Pastor Henry, now that you're ordained, next week bring a litre container of salt and I am also going to bring a container of salt. We are then both going to mix our salt together." I started laughing. He said, "the reason is when you are ready to go, I am going to bring you back the container of salt and tell you to pick your salt, from my salt." I kept laughing, as this would be impossible, and the whole thing sounded funny. The pastor went on to explain, "I am telling you this because if you leave before your time, you are going to be under a curse, because you can't pick your salt out, curses are going to follow you." At the time I really loved, respected and looked up to my pastor, however something told me 'don't do it.' So I made up my mind no matter what, I would never do what he asked me, even if there were consequences. Thankfully the pastor never brought it up again, but I realised that there had been other people who had left church and he would always say the same thing, "If you leave you are going to be under a curse, don't think I've not done it before." I wondered if he was just trying to threaten people, or if he was just being the typical African church pastor. In my experience particularly the prophetic churches, love to do that.

However, I noticed that everyone that left church, never left happy. They would warn us after they left saying, "one day you will find out about this man." I just thought they were trying to start trouble, but it was a pattern and many good people started to leave the church.

As a young believer I liked to listen to other ministers and whilst that was my home church, I did visit another local large church when they had programmes on. My then pastor was aware of this. However often when he was preaching he would chip in, "I know some of these big churches you go to, can you even speak to the pastor?" It was like he wanted to track what I was doing outside of church, and was overly critical of the choices I made.

Little by little things started to get worse, but I was blind to see the signs. Around 2015 something major happened. The pastor travelled abroad to preach for a few months. I would be preaching in the main service, in his absence and sometimes it would be the pastors wife. This would depend on how the Pastor felt, but if he wanted to raise money he would invite one of his 'prophet friends' to come and raise money. The pastor often said to me, "Pastor Henry, I wish you knew how to raise funds, cos if you did I could go to Ghana for six months and not worry about the church rent!" I was thinking, 'you want me to stand there and lie to the people? It goes against everything I believe; I am not going to do that.' I would tell the congregation that we need to raise money for the rent, but to lie to the people and say 'God is saying give a certain amount' is not what I was going to do. I was not a trickster.

During that time, I was teaching a Bible study on a Sunday and took it in turns with the pastor's wife to lead. Somehow we got onto the subject of giving. I made a comment, "let's be careful with giving, as Gods loves a cheerful giver, so let it not be under compulsion." That was the only comment I made. The pastor's wife quickly asked, "what do you mean by don't give under compulsion?" I replied and explained that sometimes some people can feel that they are being forced by the men of God to give! The moment I said that the rest of the church put their hands up declaring, "it happened to me … it happened to me!" I was wondering to myself what have I just started. We ended the Bible study and I advised that the pastors wife would continue next week. When next week arrived the conversations at Bible study carried on and everyone was complaining about prophets that came to the church. The pastor's wife did her best trying to defend them, but it was difficult. After Bible study she said I had done a good job, so I was happy and thought that was it. What I did not know was that the pastor's wife was phoning the pastor and stating that, "Henry is brainwashing the people not to give." A family member who lived with the pastors, was a close friend of mine and shared what had been said about me. When the pastor came back from his travels, I noticed he had a certain look on his face! The first Sunday he got up to preach he told the congregation, "if a man of God tells you to give, you must give. Especially if you are a leader in this church. You must get up, no matter what." I knew he was trying to get at me. Later he called me aside and expressed that he was not happy about what I did. He said, "I hear you were preaching heresy ... you brainwashed the church that they shouldn't give; that when the man of God tells them to give they should not give." We went back and forth, I wanted to know who made these accusations, as there were witnesses in the Bible study. The Pastor refused to answer, instead stated: "Because of you, I now have to rewire the mind of the people into giving." The Pastor took Bible study for the next 4 weeks and basically debunked everything I had said. Although people were still complaining, he was insistent that if people ask you to give, it really is God. I did consider leaving the church, but thought I was under persecution, and decided to stay.

In 2015 a female friend invited her friend, who had recently moved to the area, to visit our church. She had a bad experience at her previous church and was very reluctant to attend. In fact she hated church. She did eventually end up coming to church, but in less than a month the pastor was trying it on with her. There were text messages seen that evidenced his suggestive and inappropriate communication. More stories then started to come out. My ex-girlfriend had also received messages from the Pastor that were flirtatious and similar to the ones received by the other girl. People would leave church and then talk about the situations that had happened. As leaders we all became aware, and the pastor knew, that we knew. He then decided to invite one of his friends, who it seemed he had instructed, to preach about the importance of leaders covering their pastor's nakedness. They would single me out and state: "Henry be humble, some people come to the church to make trouble, some of you will fall for that, but we don't want that here." I was picked on continually, and every visiting minister that came during the next year preached a similar message.

On another occasion, during the church service the pastor had spoken to my ex-girlfriend, and asked her if she wanted to get married, and if she had someone in mind etc. He said she should see him after church. As we were still friends, she told me of this and I said, "don't go, he is going to ask you to give money." She didn't believe me, but went ahead and met with the pastor privately. He had said to her, "if you want to be with Henry give £300." She was shocked, and called me later that day with the news. I said, "it's not magic. If you want to give, give, but it won't bring me to you."

There were many incidents that happened relating to financial manipulation. The area where the church was based was notorious for gangs and drugs. We would sometimes evangelise and bring some of these individuals to church, straight off the streets. They were trying to turn their lives around, and were trying to quit selling drugs, but often after being in the church a short time they would text me and say, "why is your Pastor asking me for £200?" There was one friend in particular (who is now serving a prison sentence), who used to be in church and would share with the pastor that he was trying to stop selling drugs. But the pastor would say however, "Its ok, even me, I'm not perfect." This was because he would give the pastor drug money. This behaviour continued; single mothers, the unemployed, whoever would come to church the pastor would ask them for specific amounts of money. They would tell us what had happened after they left, but we were still so blinded, and as leaders, continued faithfully serving in church.

The following year, in 2016 my mother was very unwell and was receiving treatment. It was a very tough time for our family, but I still attended church every Sunday. I even sowed money for mums healing, and stayed committed. The whole time my mum was unwell the pastor kept saying he would visit her in hospital, but never did. He only prayed with her twice over the phone. After a few months my mum sadly passed away. The pastor did not visit and pay condolences. My friends were very upset because of that, as they saw how committed I was to the church. I had been there 10 years, and never missed a service. In fact, I opened and locked up the church and was always available to support the pastor. A week before the funeral took place my leaders at church rang and said that the pastor was very upset that I had not contacted him to update him with all the arrangements. I lost it, with all that I was going through he still had to make it about him. I went to church and could tell that the pastor had an attitude towards me. The funeral service, arranged by the elders in my community took place, and although my pastor attended, he kept his distance, staying in his car for most of the reception.

Two weeks after burying my mum, the pastor called me to his house and was complaining that I didn't introduce him to my family at the funeral, and that as a pastor I should have kept the church more involved. I couldn't believe it. He showed no compassion or understanding that I had just buried my mum. He quickly moved on and said I should open a French branch of the church. I felt like I was about to be boxed in. I said ok, but had no plans to start one, and left the meeting. In spite of everything I kept going to church, but was losing respect for my pastor. The following Sunday he was preaching about me, saying, "that some people are so precious you have to hold them like an egg."

Several months later, we had a leadership meeting and the Pastor said, "We are going to restart the church, and remember you come to church for me, not God. If I am happy with you, God is happy with you. Don't worry about your problems, especially as leaders. I will pray for your problems, so long as you make sure that I am okay." After hearing this, I decided that I was not going to stay, and began thinking about how I would leave church. The next week the pastor brought a friend to preach and generally talked about how good the pastor was.

During this time, I was dreaming daily about leaving the church, and I knew it was from God. The Lord would say, "Get out from the church, this man hates you." But I was asking the question, "When?" I am not sure why I kept going to church during that time, as it was a very toxic environment. I wonder if I stayed to escape from grieving, as it was keeping me busy, but now I had made my decision to leave.

I had told the other leaders that I was planning on leaving church the next week. There was tension amongst the other leaders too. My friend Peter was the men's leader and his wife had bought the pastor and his wife a car each, regularly paid for plane tickets, gave thousands and also had taken a loan for the church for £8000. But due to a disagreement the wife had left the church a few months previous to this. However, Peter had continued attending as he was very loyal. Before, what was to be my last service, Peter had confided in me that he had a dream where God told him to leave and start his own ministry. He was very agitated, and I advised him to pray and prepare. During service we were sat at the front of church and the pastor was preaching that 'obedience is better than sacrifice' and he said, "You guys, how many times have I told you to bring people in the church?" and also 'rebellion is as the sin of witchcraft' so if you rebel against me you are a witch! The pastor came to the leaders and began to ask each of us, "How many times have I asked you to bring people?" but when he came to Peter he responded, "I have brought people, but you don't know how to keep them!" It was a very awkward exchange and Peter was frustrated. As soon as church finished, the pastor and Peter exchanged words and to cut a long story short Peter got up and left with his children.

By this stage I was exhausted and a few days later this heaviness came over me, and I knew I couldn't step foot in the church again. I had given my time to serve over and over again, I had even lost work because of the church. Even though I was an ordained pastor I realised my life had been going backwards. That week I prayed and asked when I was meant to leave. The Lord gave me a dream and said, "leave now and don't worry about what they say." I rang the pastor and he cut me off mid-way through the conversation, stating, "If you want to leave, just leave."

We had a 12 second conversation after being in the church for 10 years! But I was relieved to finally be leaving, and becoming free. Since leaving I have heard story after story about how the pastor has preached about me, and told lies about my conduct.

In just few years after leaving the church both ministry and employment doors have opened for me. Yet this couldn't happen in the 10 long years of me being there. I had been in bondage.

The journey has been tough, but I have focused on my family, I met my now Bishop who has been supportive and encouraged me, "to do me" and was accepting of the fact that I may not be at church every week. I always knew that God had a plan for me. This has been one of my biggest motivators for healing. I would encourage others to make God's plan for their lives, their biggest motivation for healing.

CHAPTER SEVEN

Church Culture

$\mathcal{I}$t is interesting how the regular social rules and norms of society can sometimes be left at the church door. Boundaries of respect and personal space are not adhered to. Now whilst I appreciate the church is a community of love and it should be a welcoming, warm and safe environment, where do we draw the line with respecting peoples personal space? I have heard unfortunate incidences where women in church were made to feel uncomfortable by not accepting a hug and kiss (on the cheek) from older men, and the scripture that was often thrown at them was, 'Greet one another with a holy kiss'.

I believe we all have a personal choice; I remember feeling awkward in faith environments when men I didn't want to hug would hug me. A full bear hug chest to chest that felt way too intimate. I do not believe there was ill intent but it still felt too close. Too personal. Granted my mind was still full of suspicion and I had my guard up, but how do we safeguard individuals in church?

I had an awkward situation several years ago at the Bible study that I have previously mentioned. Now, I am not including this story, because I think it falls under the category of spiritual abuse, but I include it because it shows how behaviour unchecked and boundaries untested have the possibility of escalating. Also how easily this incident could have caused me to retreat and been another nail in the coffin of being dead to church, dead to Christians, and dead to fellowship. I'll say it over and over again, the saving grace for my story is that I had a personal relationship with Jesus, that meant come what may I will find my way back to truth, as He has me, but it's not the same for everyone.

Damage is deep, damage can penetrate the soul of an individual to unimaginable levels. When you add damage from church brethren to an already fragile, unsupported and weakened soul its impact is far greater. The term 'trigger' is a word I have used a few times, but generally do not like. Partly because it's almost overused out of context, however the concept is very real. What might seemingly be an innocent touch can actually trigger someone else, it might cause a flashback to a previous situation, a painful incident or an uncomfortable memory.

Am I saying we should all walk around on egg shells? No! Am I saying we don't interact with brethren and demonstrate love and care? No! Am I saying we police gatherings and enforce strict "rules"? No. What I am saying is that we create a culture of safety and mutual respect. I am saying we teach people that someone can politely refuse a hug, for example, without the initiator being offended. I am saying that we make it known that if anyone has concerns they can speak to leadership. I am saying that if certain behaviours are noticed and seem inappropriate we don't "just" pray about it. We pray about it and take appropriate action.

Recently someone confided in me, that she had been

approached and improperly touched by a married man in her church, and this was not the first time. She has contacted the leadership team, and although the man was spoken to, he was allowed to carry on in his ministry roles as normal, with the hope that he will be changed and restored!!! The frustration that arose in my gut was real. Restoration at what cost? I pray wisdom for church leaders who have to take care of their sheep, whilst tending to individual needs, whilst not sitting back and watching other sheep be damaged in the process. This individual has a supportive husband, who she made aware and he also spoke to the man in question, but there has to be a better way. If she was timid, if she was scared, if she felt powerless there is no telling where the story could have led.

So what happened to me?

As mentioned it was a Bible study I used to go to, there were attendees from different churches and for several years this was my safe place. I was attending through the transition from the Eden House to my new church. I had learnt truths upon truths upon truths that were impacting me at Bible study. I was taught how to practically not just hear the word but apply the word. How to allow the ancient and timeless Word of God to translate from the pages into me. Into my thought life, into my behaviour, and into my decisions. It brought clarity and revelation that was not always easy or pain free but it was also life changing. Therefore, going to Bible study was not just like popping into a regular meeting, it meant a lot to me, and as stated earlier it was a safe place.

On this particular evening Bible Study finished as usual with prayer, and we all said goodbye, the attendees often hugged and kissed each other on the cheek. As I was hugging one of the older gentlemen he proceeded to 'munch' on my cheek. Now when I use the word munch I am talking about what a parent may do to a young baby, often to show affection and make them laugh. It's like you are pretending to eat the baby's face, but not using teeth. It's something I'm sure you may have done to your own children, grandchildren, nieces or nephews. It's an expression of love, its playful, fun and very young children enjoy it. It's innocent. However there has to be a relational basis for this type of affection. It would be deemed incredibly inappropriate to go up to a stranger's baby and munch them, never mind the safeguarding and hygiene aspects, since you don't actually know that person! So you can imagine my shock as an adult to have my cheek 'munched' on by a man at Bible Study. He was not someone I was really close to and we had no contact outside the Bible study.

The interesting thing about hindsight, once again, is that you have the perfect response, and the perfect words to speak. But in that moment I was so shocked, I froze. I couldn't say or do anything. Yes, I felt violated, but I was stunned into silence and couldn't quite believe what happened did actually happen. On my way home I shared with a friend who also attended Bible study what had occurred, the leadership was made aware, the gentleman was spoken to. By the next week I received an apology. I am thankful for the way in which the situation was handled, but it did mean that on some level, and with the backdrop of my painful past, I no longer felt as 'safe' at Bible Study. The situation had somehow raised my defensive wall once again.

I do not believe this was a situation of spiritual abuse. It was inappropriate, and I do not think the gentlemen had malice towards me. He crossed boundaries and became too familiar. From the outside looking in, it can be easy to judge a situation and victim blame about why they didn't speak up at the time or challenge the behaviour. But until you are in the same situation, having the same historical experiences, it can be very difficult to understand. Unchecked it is situations like these that can, over time, escalate and become abusive causing some people to leave church altogether.

I greatly respect the leadership of the Bible study for listening, believing and addressing the situation swiftly. There are many other cases where the individuals share what has happened, raise concerns and are not believed, or everything is just swept under the carpet and excuses for the person are given. It is apparent there can be a toxic culture where everything must be hidden as "we don't want to rock the boat" or worse still (in my humble opinion) is that the individuals are questioned to find out what they did to cause this situation. Maybe never out rightly stating blame, but implying it. How tragic that someone plucks up the courage to share what has happened and rather than a listening and understanding ear, they are met with criticism and suspicion; because "that doesn't sound like the sister or brother so and so that I know". Leaders, may we listen without jumping to conclusion, listen to learn and exercise wisdom and Godly counsel to address matters.

Nell T's Story

It was the Autumn of 2011. I had been church hopping for a while, seeking somewhere to belong. Then I came across what seemed like a modern vibrant church; they put on hip hop concerts for the youth and had broken away from many traditional 'old school' church culture. The pastor and his wife seemed friendly; they were young, good looking and had just moved to the area to plant this church.

The pastors were keen to encourage the congregation to be involved in the ministry. I had never done this before but at first I was happy to sit back as an observer. The church was very much performance based and was focused on outward appearances. For example, how you behaved in church; whether you smiled, raised your hands in worship etc. It felt like a good show had to be put on, and there was little emphasis based on your own authentic journey of faith.

After a few months it soon became evident that I was not meeting their standards, as in my ability to 'put on a show.' I was told I wasn't smiling enough and not actively involved in ministry, which was the expectation for all whether they were gifted or not. Members of the church would have get-togethers and not invite me. I began to feel excluded, but eventually I complied with their wishes and started volunteering and getting involved in the ministry.

I began going out evangelising, handing out flyers on the street. At this stage I was in my early 30s and I began to feel quite old as they liked to target the youth through their hip hop concerts. I eventually started using my talents and would sing and choreograph dances in the children's church. It was nice to feel part of something; we were like a family. Because, I was now "conforming" I found that people would invite me out and I in return would open my home to them to have fellowship. During one church service I received a prophecy publicly and interestingly it seemed like I was now "approved" and therefore even more welcome. Things were great until I started to come under surveillance.

On one occasion the pastor called me into his office, he explained that someone from church saw me going into the cinema the other day. I advised that although it was secular it was a standard PG film, I even took my daughter. He said in a patronising tone, "sister you can't be in ministry and going to those sort of places." I was shocked but this was just the start of many events that caused me to question my position in the church.

Woe betide you if you missed a bible study or service, you were accused of backsliding and would face a full interrogation. I thought to myself what kind of bondage is this?

Church became a hostile environment - whereby if you did not have your church game you were not welcomed. So I learned to be an actress for a while for the sake of complying.

The pastor also took issue with certain books I read, especially if they were from Joyce Meyer / TD Jakes etc. He encouraged members to consult him before making certain purchases and decisions i.e. which books to read, where to go on holiday etc. They would state that going to visit other churches was like contracting STD's. Unbeknown to me they followed a 'shepherding' theology. I continued reading what I wanted but did not make it known to the church or pastors.

The church insisted on open confession and wanted me to tell them all about my past. There were some occasions I confided in the pastor's wife, but the next thing I knew I was being made an example of from the pulpit. They betrayed my trust completely and I thought 'how dare you ...' Incidents like these served as a warning to the congregation not to disobey the leader.

I found it all a bit strange so I just became more secretive, as I lacked trust and felt things were not right. Things came to a head when I was called into Pastor's office for the umpteenth time and I wondered what I had done this time. He said I was unteachable and rebellious, he said he had noticed that I was not smiling as much and not sitting at the front of the church and this was a poor witness. I left his office feeling like a scolded child.

I became withdrawn and depressed. During that season I called out to God; I pondered surely Christianity was not supposed to be like this, I felt burdened. God began to teach me about grace, I had never understood the concept before. I was only used to fire and brimstone teaching. I found it fascinating and began researching and reading scripture, seeking God for myself.

It was great for my spiritual development but of course my new insights were not welcomed in the church. They did not like anyone to visit other churches or organisations.

I was going through a challenging time personally within my marriage and went to Pastor for counsel. He told me to divorce my then husband, which I did. Years later I asked him why he told me to divorce, he replied "I told you what you wanted to hear". I regret going off his decision, as at the time I thought he was listening to the Holy Spirit.

I later realised that they believed that if you were single and unmarried then the pastor can act as your husband to be a covering. The one who you had to check in with about every decision; i.e. asking where I am going, what I am doing and being answerable. However, he sent people to follow me and watch what I was doing. He stated he was there to protect me.

When I began asking questions about free will, grace, the wilderness experience, tithes and offerings, other members would report me and when I posed the same questions to the leader I was quickly silenced. Apart from a couple of good friends the majority of the congregation began to distance themselves from me.

Eventually I explained to pastor that I felt certain things were not lining up with what the scriptures said and I asked him if indeed I am misguided please pray for me as I want to know the truth. He looked at me and shook his head and said "No, I won't pray for you, maybe this is not the church for you. Perhaps you should go to a more mature church."

Still in disbelief I said OK and told him this will be my final week. I said my goodbyes and left as quickly as I could.

What hurt was that in the months and years to follow I would see people from the church in the local shopping centre and they would blatantly blank me. I felt a sense of alienation, loneliness and disillusionment

I do not necessarily think they are bad people; they just have a misguided loyalty to their pastor. Overall this whole experience drew me closer to God but also caused me to be increasingly cynical about the church. I struggled to find a place of belonging when going to church after that.

I went through various grieving stages as it was like a loss. I was hurt and angry initially. I thought how dare they abuse people in the name of God. I felt foolish to have been duped and so desperate for affection.

I stayed in that church for several years because I did not want to be disrespectful. I thought I was perhaps too carnal and that's why I was having these issues. I was also frequently reminded ' do not touch my anointed ones, do, them no harm' (Psalm 105.15). I didn't want to be guilty of that, or my salvation to be questioned.

For a long time, I did not want to go to church or get close to anyone, and sometimes those old feelings would creep back. However, I have to lay them down at the altar and walk in the revelations that God has given me.

Spiritual Abuse And The Law

Disclaimer, whilst I am sharing my story and the stories of others there is the huge issue of spiritual abuse and the law, which I am not going to address here. So this is a section to explain why I have chosen not to address it. A quick Google search will find that there are other books, resources and individuals far more knowledgeable and experienced than I am, on the subject of spiritual abuse.

Like many other forms of abuse, spiritual abuse, may not tidily and neatly fit under one legislation that evidences a law has been broken, or that any criminal activity has taken place. In many incidences it could be argued that nothing "illegal" or criminal has happened as the survivors willingly; did, sold, gave, stated and the list goes on. To "evidence" fear, control and manipulation is tough, and for most individuals they themselves believe that everything is well, above board and even Godly and pleasing to the heavens.

There are some cases where it is very apparent a crime has been committed and a law broken, and I would encourage survivors to seek legal advice to have those further conversations.

I am sure you are familiar with the phrase "prevention is better than cure,' and by speaking up, sharing our stories and reporting the matter to relevant authorities, in some way we can help prevent spiritual abuse from happening to other people. I have come to the resolve that not everyone will believe all our stories, and that is perfectly okay. Maybe you find yourself in a position, where you are trying to "prove" that what you experienced, really did happen. I appreciate that this can be exhausting; let me remind you that it is okay.

Amos 5:24 states:

> *But let justice run down like water, And righteousness like a mighty stream.*

Amos 5:24 NKJV

It is important to realise that nothing that happens to us, in any aspect of our lives, goes unseen by the Omnipotent and Omnipresent God that we serve. Whilst our experiences, as survivors of spiritual abuse, have been tough, and at times unbearable, we are assured that provision has already been made for our complete healing through Jesus Christ.

CHAPTER Eight

The Power of Healing & forgiveness

"As hard as forgiveness can be, it is liberating and freeing"
Apostle Elijah Chanak

*H*ealing is understood to be the process of making or becoming sound, better, healthy or whole. In the Bible healing sometimes happened instantly, at other times it happened in stages, or in other words the healing was a process. Your personal healing journey will be unique to you; it will come in a time frame unique to you, and in an order that is unique to you. And it will also be your choice whether you choose to undergo this healing process. You may not know exactly what you need healing from or the type of healing that you need. Have faith that the Lord does know. You just have to make up in your mind that you desire this.

Jesus always wants to heal the broken and the crushed. He invites us to come to Him. In John 5:6 we are told:

> When Jesus saw him lying there, and knew that he already had been in that condition a long time, He said to him, "Do you want to be made well?

John 5:6 NKJV

There is no set formula for healing, however there are some fundamentals, and I would argue that forgiveness is one of these. This is a vital process for any believer who has been spiritually abused or have found themselves in a spiritually abusive and harmful environment. This may seem hard; near impossible BUT it is possible!

Many who have been wounded, harmed and damaged often feel that forgiveness is not fair. Let's just get that out there; you may never have said that statement aloud to anyone, but let's be real! How many of us believe this to be true? Forgiveness is not fair! No, it is not fair. Neither is it rational, reasonable or just. How could it be that if someone makes a serious mistake; if they hurt someone, whether intentionally or even accidentally, that they are forgiven?

How is it fair that they can be pardoned or excused for the wrong that they have done? That when they acknowledge or confess; say sorry to God and repent, that they are forgiven. It is not fair that when someone does wrong, then obeys Gods word in asking for forgiveness, that they are forgiven.

Transgressions; sin, wrongs. It is not rational or reasonable that they should be given a second, third, fifth, or even thirty fifth chance. After all you would have thought that after making mistakes for long enough they would really know better, but still they mess up.

Whilst it may not seem 'fair,' the truth of the matter is that each and every one of us, have at times done something wrong, that required forgiveness. Whether from other people or from God. If we hang onto the notion that forgiveness is not fair when others wrong us, then that same principle must also apply to us in our wrongdoing. That is a very sobering thought.

The Bible says in Romans 3:23 that:

All have sinned and fallen short of the glory of God.

Romans 3:23 KJV

Yes, even the seemingly most holy, pure, righteous, prayerful "perfect" person that you know, admire and possibly even a teeny bit envy, has done something wrong that required forgiveness! Human beings sin in different ways but it is all sin. Can you imagine if there was no hope of forgiveness? It would be a pretty dire and desperate situation.

We are each afforded the privilege of forgiveness, it may not seem fair – reasonable or rationale, BUT it is evidence of the mercy, kindness, goodness and provision of God.

It is because of this truth that as children of God we must extend forgiveness to those who have hurt, harmed and damaged us. It has nothing to do with fairness, but it has everything to do with Gods mercy and grace. As demonstrated through the birth, death, burial and resurrection of Jesus Christ. He is our greatest example of love and forgiveness for the undeserving. In Luke 23:34 we are told:

> *Then said Jesus, Father, forgive them; for they know not what they do. And they parted his raiment, and cast lots.*
>
> Luke 23:34 KJV

I do not think it helpful, to attempt to 'compare' the size of the sin, or number of wrongs that has been committed against us. They are equally painful, they are equally harmful, and are all damaging. Our experiences of pain may differ, depending on the intricate complexities of experience, history and many other factors. Therefore, we must never trivialise another person's experiences, as this can only add to their pain. We can never see it from the other person's perspective because it was their experience, and it was their pain.

When we consider the life of Jesus we see that he was betrayed, arrested, falsely accused, imprisoned and beaten. He was stripped, lashed and had his beard plucked out. He had thorns dug in his skull and had huge nails driven into his hands and his feet. He was then hung on a cross. Despite all of this, in the midst of horrific pain, Jesus still CHOSE to forgive. Jesus made a choice, a conscious act of His will to forgive those who crucified Him. He forgave them, without them asking for forgiveness, Jesus spoke those words out loud, then He died.

So the first truth we learn here is that forgiveness is a choice that we have to make. Because we have been forgiven, we also have to forgive.

+ Choose to forgive those who harmed you, hurt you, misused and abused you.

+ Choose to forgive those who perhaps suspected or knew something was wrong but did nothing.

+ Choose to forgive yourself for any part you may have played in the matter.

Forgiveness is not conditional. It is not based on whether somebody acknowledges they have done wrong and says sorry. This was an aspect that I really struggled with personally. I felt that if there was no admission on their part, about what happened to me, it was as though they simply 'got away with it.' I struggled with wondering whether other leaders knew about the 'sin offering,' and if they did know, how come they did not do or say anything? I was too broken to even approach them. Part of the heartbreak was that no acknowledgment, categorically meant no apology for what happened. In some way I felt that I 'needed' the wrong done to be acknowledged.

The truth is I did not, and neither do you. Forgiveness is for you. Nobody else but you. It is between you and God and in that way, acknowledgement from the perpetrator(s) is not really necessary.

I do believe that, where possible, the situation of the wrong does need to be addressed and the appropriate body made aware. This is important because it may help safeguard other individuals. In any case I would urge you to seek counsel. Addressing the situation is not for the purpose of demanding an apology, rather it is to bring light to the situation.

Sometimes, we may believe that leaders and individuals who have caused us harm, will somehow be able to soothe our wounds with their words of apology. But even if an apology does happen, it is not always easy to receive, as the trust has already been broken. Also leaders and individuals who have caused harm may never know the full extent of the damage inflicted by their actions and behaviour. As such any apology would never fully satisfy the depth of the damage caused.

This brings us to a number of questions, concerning the forgiveness of spiritual abuse, which need to be considered:

1. Is there a belief that leaders and individuals who have caused harm to others are able to take full responsibility?

2. Are they honest enough to recognise and acknowledge that they have done wrong?

3. Are they ever repentant and willing to right the many wrongs they have done?

Possibly in some circumstances, but certainly not all.

Have you ever thought how much more damage could be inflicted if everything that happened to you was denied?

If those who harmed you, whether consciously or unconsciously, swore that what you said happened and how you have been affected by it, was a lie?

Forgiveness is possible without acknowledgement. Without hearing the words 'I am sorry.' Jesus demonstrated this. I would implore you to pour out your pain to the Lord and choose to forgive even without hearing 'I am sorry.'

On my journey into the place of forgiveness, I have personally had to accept that the Lord is my vindicator. I have had to learn that vindication could never come through the hands of those who spiritually abused me. It took much prayer and consistently choosing to forgive, to achieve my freedom in Christ.

Freedom brought greater deliverance and helped the healing process.

Jesus Confessed His Forgiveness Out Loud.

Have you ever questioned the integrity of your own thoughts? Have you ever questioned whether the decision you made to forgive was authentic? If so, this can be answered when your statement of forgiveness is declared out loud. The declaration 'I choose to forgive' takes on greater resonance when you can actually hear yourself saying it. I had to do this time and time again, in my personal prayer time, and also when I had counselling and prayer ministry.

I recall for years being unable to say the name of the pastors and key people involved in what I experienced. I was even unable to say the name 'Eden House'. A few years ago I had sadly lost a family member and through my work, telephone counselling sessions had been arranged. This was put in place to support me in my grieving process. At the first session, the counsellor introduced themselves, and ironically they shared the exact same name as one of the leaders from the church. Well that was the end of being able to have a conversation about my current grief, and the beginning of a conversation about that individual, and the complexities of what I thought and felt about what I had suffered.

In a video I recorded on the subject of forgiveness, I described it as an invisible string. An invisible string that connects a wound in our body to the person who inflicted that wound on us and caused us the pain. I further explained as the years go by and more hurtful and harmful situations occur, more wounds are created. Each of these wounds have their own invisible string attached to different people. Imagine you are trying to live life and yet all of these strings are attaching the hurt and damaged parts of you to countless others. It is not only restricting and suffocating, but also it is a constant reminder of 'what they did'. This poses a grim picture right? Here we are trying to navigate the complexities of life's seasons; trying to grow, trying to change. Yet these strings keep us pulled in every direction and the pain ever so present. We can try and use some form of pain relief, however it is only ever a temporary fix. As time moves on, people move on, and so we want and desire to also move on. Yet we find that we cannot.

We find ourselves stuck ... stagnant ... stapled to the memories of all the wrong. Before long this stuck-ness and stagnation becomes our norm. It becomes all that we know and then what we expect. In a twisted way we grow into the discomfort, but strangely familiarity of this stuck season. It becomes who we are, or more accurately, who we think we are. After all, if you tell yourself the same thing over and over and over for long enough, it eventually becomes your truth. Irrespective of the origins, root or nature of that thing. Can you relate to this?

Maybe you recognise in yourself or in a loved one a cycle of stagnancy. A cycle of pain and frustration. Are you or a loved one talking about the past continuously? But never for the purpose of testifying a victory, or a tale of overcoming, but instead a constant rehearsal of the pain! Bear with me as I precisely and intently encourage you to put a wedge in this cycle.

It does not have to be this way. It does not have to be the way it has always been. It does not have to be this way now or in the future. Change is possible. I would strongly encourage you to allow the Lord to walk you through your healing journey. Do not focus only on your feelings, because they may take a while to catch up to your choices. It is ok if you do not 'feel' like you have forgiven, when you have, simply believe that you have. It may take you saying, "I forgive you." several times, and that is perfectly OK

I must confess that this may not be an easy, enjoyable or pain free journey of forgiveness. HOWEVER, it will be one of the best journeys you will ever take. You will find freedom and it marks the end of a chapter and the beginning of your next chapter entitled wholeness.

Again forgiveness is a process. We read in scripture:

> Then Peter came to Him and said, "Lord, how often shall my brother sin against me, and I forgive him? Up to seven times?" Jesus said to him, "I do not say to you, up to seven times, but up to seventy times seven."

Matthew 18:21-22 NKJV

Forgive. Forgive unconditionally. Forgive repeatedly. Continue to confess that you forgive out loud.

Bethany K's Story

Our father which art in heaven, Hallowed be thy name. Thy kingdom come. Thy will be done in earth, as it is in heaven. Give us this day our daily bread. And forgive us our debts, as we forgive our debtors. And lead us not into temptation, but deliver us from evil: For thine is the kingdom, and the power, and the glory, forever. Amen.

Matthew 6:9-13

I lived by this Matthew chapter 6 scripture, in which we are taught to forgive, so that we can be forgiven, or so I thought. We are encouraged in the bible to examine ourselves, and over the years had I examined myself thoroughly in line with the word of God, I would have discovered that there were still many layers of unforgiveness in my heart. These many layers were relating to issues and situations that I had not yet surrendered upon the altar of forgiveness, so that I could truly forgive those concerned.

We are taught in Matthew 6:15:

> *But if ye forgive not men their trespasses, neither will your Father forgive your trespasses.*

Matthew 6:15 KJV

There are many instances where God, by the power of the holy spirit, had to show me the error of my ways, and how I had buried many things in my heart, rather that truly forgive.

It is so easy to love those who love us; to love the ones who are good to us. It is so easy to love those who are in our clique, and the ones who look and sound just like us. It is good to remember however, that true love does not have a criterion. It does not have a shape or colour, and neither does it have any restrictions, except the ones we choose to build around it. Often built through hurts, but sometimes through ignorance, selfishness or narrow-mindedness. We often choose to withhold love, rather than give it away.

A significant opportunity to demonstrate the power of forgiveness came about through my association with the leadership in one of my previous churches. The incident coincided with a period in my life when our family fell on hard times. We went from a place of plenty to a place of lack, and I felt shame and embarrassment that I found myself there. A place where I had to carefully and precisely calculate before spending anything. At the time I was head of administration at my church. This role included taking minutes at leadership meetings and disseminating information, via email to the team, as well as maintaining various weekly rotas.

At that time, I had no access to the internet nor did I have any printing facilities. I was unable to personally fund and print material for distribution within the church and email access was limited. I had confided in Charlie, one of the leaders some of the particulars of my then situation and restricted facilities. Charlie also worked in an advisory capacity within the church. Over the years we had established a friendship; I had respect for him and he was one of the leaders I had grown to trust. I felt that with Charlie knowing my predicament prior to one of our regular leadership meetings, he would help figure out a way to move forward, in relation to the smooth running of the administration of the church. I also believed Charlie would do so, without the discomfort of me having to share my personal circumstances to the whole room. In fact, I had no doubt that he would back me up one hundred percent, employing diplomacy and discretion regarding my situation.

The evening of the leadership meeting came and to my shock Charlie behaved totally out of character. He turned on me in a manner that can only be described as vicious. Charlie began to grill me in front of the whole room, and it felt as though he was the prosecutor and I was the accused. He was insistent that I tell the other leaders exactly how I was going to carry out my role and distribute the material as necessary. I felt both shocked and humiliated. It was as though my face was on fire, he was asking me questions, that I did not know how to answer, because at that time I had no answers. It was as if I was being exposed and I felt very vulnerable. Here I was, a woman, everyone in church assumed was doing well in life and could handle the administrative tasks competently, but my situation had changed. I was confused about Charlie's behaviour, and did not understand what was happening. The remainder of the discussions became a blur to me. I do not remember to this day what transpired in the rest of the meeting.

As I was driving home, hot tears were falling down my cheeks. I felt betrayed and my trust had been broken. I decided that I was done with the church and the leaders. I felt ganged up on. I was offering my services and my expertise free of charge to the church. I was helping to raise the standard of how we operated, and what had just transpired did not seem like a fair exchange to me. The tears kept falling, and I felt so overwhelmed that I was forced to pull my car over on the side of the road and just cry. I did not want my husband to see the evidence of tears when I got home. He was not a believer at the time and this situation would not have boded well with him. To make matters worse, I was also one of the women's ministry leaders, and there was a scheduled breakfast event taking place the very next morning. Because of what had just happened to me, I made the decision to stay at home and not attend.

The next morning when I was in bed preparing to have a lie-in, I heard the spirit of God say words to this effect, "Get out of bed and go to the breakfast meeting." The voice was so strong that I immediately got up, showered, dressed and left the house. As I was getting ready I kept wondering whether God was able to see and hear the things I had experienced. I felt emotionally bruised and psychologically wounded. Somehow, however, I got through the event and it was in giving of myself and serving the women at the meeting that morning, that I received temporary relief from the hurt, caused by the events of the previous evening.

I had a keen sense of justice and so at every opportunity I would bring Charlie and the matter before God. I kept complaining to God about what Charlie had done to me. Instead of empathising with me God said that I should start to pray for Charlie and to bless him! Surprised and albeit reluctantly, I started to obey the instructions I was given, but it was an offering of mere words without any meaning or substance to them. Sometimes I would explain to God that I was the wronged one, yet here I was being asked to pray for the perpetrator. None of it made sense to me. Another time God told me that I had to humble myself. I then saw a vision of two men standing in a boxing ring, and here I was taught something vital.

Both boxers were standing eye ball to eye ball, punches were then thrown, and someone would get hurt; but as soon as one boxer fell to his knees, the blows would stop. Being on your knees is a humble position. In that moment the one standing appears to be the stronger one because they were the one throwing the blows, and seemingly winning. God taught me, however, that living a life of humility before Him is like being on your knees in a stance of total and continual surrender. There is not always the need to square up to someone else and defend your position. Being on your knees figuratively, is a position of great strength for *the believer. Real strength is found in choosing not to hurt those who hurt you. It is choosing to give up your right to be right. This is a hard thing, but it leads to the way of peace.*

I kept on praying for Charlie, and one day the Lord gave me a scripture: it was from the book of Psalms which said God was my vindicator. I believe the Lord was saying that if I remained obedient and prayed for those who hurt and abused me, He would vindicate me. It was during one of those times that I was praying for Charlie that something unexpected happened. For the first time I suddenly felt moved with compassion for Charlie and as I prayed, a tear pricked my eye. What had started as mere words on my lips had finally reached my heart, and in that moment, I realised that I had totally forgiven Charlie. My prayers for him were now coming from my heart. Ephesians 4:32: 'And be ye kind one to another, tenderhearted, forgiving one another, even as God for Christ's sake hath forgiven you.'

The process of forgiveness and healing where Charlie was concerned had run its course. I realised on reflection that I had totally forgotten the offence. Charlie and his family had continued to attend the church but after a while they left, and we remained in contact. One day Charlie and his family invited me over for a meal. It was a very pleasant evening of sharing and fellowship, and I enjoyed catching up with them and hearing how well they were all doing. At the end of the evening, as I was being shown to the door, Charlie turned to me and said, "you remember the incident that took place at that leadership meeting, I am sorry." I was surprised to hear him say that, as two years had passed. I knew it had to be God as it was so unexpected. I told Charlie, 'it was okay.' Not only had I already forgiven him for what he had done, but I had also forgotten what the Lord had said about vindicating me.

In Psalm chapter 7 we learn that we can call upon Jehovah God as our vindicator. He is a just and righteous God and He is fair. He uses what happens to us to teach us truths, which have eternal value.

The truth, as I now understand it, is that unforgiveness does more harm to the unforgiving one, than it does to the one who had caused the offense. The truth is when we are hurt, we should run to forgive the person as soon as possible. Do so before the offense seeps into the pores and into the heart, where it can do untold damage. We are very aware that the devil comes but to kill, steal and destroy. Jesus came however, that we would have life and life more abundantly, John 10:10. Walking in unforgiveness is clearly not walking in life abundant. When an individual hurt us, unless we are able to forgive quickly, every time we remember what they did; every time we dwell on it, we are subconsciously, choosing to continue the negative work they started. In other words, the person may have hurt us once or twice, but then we are actually multiplying the hurt. We do so according to the number of days, months or even years that we choose to hang on to the unforgiveness and hurt within in our hearts. What is so tragic about this is that often the offender or the perpetrator has long forgotten about the incident and has moved on with their life.

The wounded one however becomes stuck in the incident.

We should refuse to live a conditional life based on what has happened to us. We should choose not to allow offence to determine how we behave, what we say and where we go. When we do so, we are actually giving away our power; we become someone else and the offender wins. When we, however, choose to forgive and let go, we are breaking their hold over us. Our decision must be to walk free no matter the cost. We must not let the enemy win because it is too costly emotionally, psychologically, spiritually and even physically. We must call on the name of the Lord and engage heaven in the healing process.

I read somewhere that forgiveness is not some psychological trick. Rather it is a miracle, and for the most severely hurt, wounded and damaged this miracle can only be done with the help of Almighty God. It is clear, then, that the wounded and hurt individual does not always of themselves have the capacity to forgive, unless they receive divine enablement to do. The healing process begins in earnest with arriving at the place of total surrender and yielding of the self and the will to the ways and will of Jehovah God, our heavenly father.

Our Father which art in heaven, Hallowed be thy name. Thy kingdom come. Thy will be done in earth, as it is in heaven. Give us this day our daily bread. And forgive us our debts, as we forgive our debtors. And lead us not into temptation, but deliver us from evil: For thine is the kingdom, and the power, and the glory, forever. Amen

Does forgiveness always mean restoration?

In my experience something that can be a struggle when it comes to forgiveness is the notion or understanding that once you have forgiven, everything goes back to 'normal'. I do not believe that this is always the case. Forgiveness is about you choosing to release the wrong and no longer hold that person(s) in a place of judgement. Your safety and wellbeing is paramount, and to return or even remain in a spiritually toxic and abusive environment is unhealthy. Healing and wholeness is hard if you are continually experiencing spiritual abuse. You forgive one incident, get healed, only for another one to be inflicted is a very dangerous cycle. I would implore you to use wisdom to make the right decision and receive the right counsel. Just to reiterate, because you have forgiven, this does not mean you have to go back to play "happy church families" in order to 'prove' you have forgiven. Forgiveness does not always mean restoration of the relationship.

CHAPTER NINE

Healing and Redemption

*"What has happened to you may not be your fault,
but who you are is your responsibility, irrespective of
who hurts you, who dishonours you, who betrays you
and who devalues you, maintain your standards."*

Apostle Elijah Chanak

*M*y journey of healing and restoration has been a rewarding, soul satisfying and life changing journey. Whilst also being painful, challenging and hard. Despite this, there is truly nothing more painful than staying stuck in a wounded place or toxic environment. I am not speaking just about the physical but also the mental and emotional. It is important that you know that you are worth all of the effort it takes to embark on this journey of healing.

I wonder what you see when you look in the mirror? Whether you see a reflection of who you really are, or whether you see what other people have said about you. Do you see how they have treated you, misused you and called you something less than God intended? The Bible says that the enemy is the father of lies. (John 8:44b) So often other people can be a tool in the hands of the enemy. They label us with their lies; they attack our future, our purpose and ultimately our identity. Lies and half-truths are shrouded in darkness and deception. However, when you are in the light it is easier to discern what is of darkness.

Conversely when we are in the dark, it is impossible to distinguish what resides in that same darkness.

I come with truth, with the good news that it is Jesus (not church, not leaders, not religious services, neither is it rules and regulations) but Jesus Christ, son of the living God. He is the One who died and rose again to bring reconciliation, redemption and righteousness to you and I. He is the One who is the ultimate source; the healer and the restorer. He is the way, the truth and the life. Outside of Christ we will only ever receive a measure; a watered down dose of healing and restoration, but in Him is complete wholeness. One of the names of God in Hebrew is Jehovah Rapha, the God who heals. This means both healing and wholeness. This is the way it was designed to be. That is what we want; to function fully and function in wholeness. God is a beautiful orchestrator of people, events, times and situations and He will indeed use people, leaders and church to help us along the journey.

My journey to wholeness and restoration from spiritual abuse has taken some years but I believe I am there now, by the grace of God. I am free to love, live and be me. The me that God destined and ordained before the foundation of the world. I am perfectly imperfect in Christ.

We will shortly take a closer look at some specific areas that the spiritual abuse impacted, and what the healing looked like. Each of our journeys will look different, and will be in a different order. The golden thread that should run throughout is a willingness from you. A willingness to be willing and available to go on that healing journey. A willingness to 'go there;' to allow the most painful areas to be unwrapped and exposed as if on the operating table. A medical doctor has to see a wounded area in the light to get a good look. They use different medical instruments, particular to the wound and they use differing processes to aid the healing. Exposure and cleansing are part of the process. Every dead; rotten, foreign and infectious thing has to be removed for healing to take place. There may be some prodding to get down to the deep areas; some peeling back layers to see what is really at the core may be necessary. It may be temporarily uncomfortable, sore and painful, but as I mentioned previously the journey is worth it, because you are worth it.

Like many survivors of spiritual abuse, I had no idea that what I had experienced was indeed spiritual abuse. Furthermore, I had no idea of the ramifications of this, and how it had impacted so many areas of my life. Over the years the Lord has allowed me to understand the reasons why I had developed certain behaviour patterns and why I reacted in particular ways.

These revelations sometimes came about whilst I was in prayer. Other times they came through books, teachings and personal insight. However, the most common ways these revelations came about was through my interactions with other people. Certain individuals were particularly graced in this season, to be able to handle me and my many issues. I lived offended and it was often those closest to me who bore the brunt of that offense. I was so wrapped in wounded-ness that I simply could not see the truth. What would often happen was that they would mention, or do something, maybe even challenge me about a particular thing, most would consider normal. However, my reactions were usually extreme, because unbeknown to me they were touching a sensitive area of a historic wound. At times I shocked myself with the level of hurt that I felt, which manifested as anger, rage and defensiveness. Although it was those closest to me, who saw me in these raw and vulnerable moments, I can truly declare that God is a deliverer and a healer. I did what I needed to do. I forgave and became intentional about my healing. This often came about as a result of my obedience to the instruction of the Holy Spirit. I attended counselling, journalled and received prayer ministry along the journey. Also ensuring that I attended church regularly; growing in my personal relationship with the Lord.

Over the years I have come to realise that these are the main areas that the spiritual abuse I encountered had the most impact: -

+ **Scepticism About Church Leaders**

This was a colossal one. As I have journeyed through my healing, I have learnt how to replace my scepticism with discernment. If something seems 'off' it pretty much usually is. But yes, I was super sceptical about pastors particularly. I silently questioned their motives; silently questioned the "on stage act" and felt that church leaders were my least favourite people. Now, I absolutely get that all pastors are human beings, and for that reason they are imperfect people. There are, however, character traits that determine their standards, ethics and beliefs. After I left Eden House and started attending my new church, I was subconsciously waiting for the leaders to mess up! Seriously, in my view, it was just a matter of time, and I would be proved right. That in fact, all pastors and leaders have an agenda and their motivation is to ensure that church works for them. In particular how the congregation can serve them and their needs! This was something I thought about the leaders in my own church, and also other churches I visited. I almost wince at the thought of my attitude, but pain is a distorter.

Since that time, I have attended service, after service over the years and I have been proved wrong concerning my previous beliefs. I saw with my very own eyes the evidence that not all pastors are the same; that not all leaders have the same heart. It is easy to be told something, and it can make a difference, but to actually experience it, in high definition, bold colour and cinematic sound is transformational. I have, and continue to experience genuinely caring; loving, Spirit filled, servant leaders. I never knew that this was possible.

Shortly after leaving Eden House, whilst still in the midst of my brokenness, I was led to this scripture in Jeremiah:

> "Return, O backsliding children," says the Lord; "for I am married to you. I will take you, one from a city and two from a family, and I will bring you to Zion. And I will give you shepherds according to My heart, who will feed you with knowledge and understanding."
>
> Jeremiah 3:14-15 NKJV

At the time I was church-less and grieving the loss of close relationships, Yet, in the midst of everything, God's word came as promise. A promise of healing; a reminder of truth and hope for a good shepherd. This word came as an instruction to return and not allow myself to 'slide away!' It came as a promise of what was to come. I dutifully journalled my thoughts, and I have seen, over the years, these promises manifest as truth.

There are other ministers in my life, who I have encountered through the dance ministry and family connections, who have also practically demonstrated love. That they have my best interests at heart, without any ulterior motives or hidden agendas. This has been incredibly healing. If any of what I have shared resonates with you, please believe me when I say that there ARE good leaders out there. Leaders who will care about you with no strings attached, and no ulterior motives. I pray you will be led to encounter them, in the areas of your life where you need it most.

I am no longer sceptical about church leaders.

◆ Serving And Ministering In The Church

I was used to serving in church. In fact, mostly serving, and whilst I did it with a willing heart, I also began to unknowingly attach my worth to serving and I became performance driven! I could not understand what my faith and church life should look like without having a role or three to do. However, I initially did nothing in my new church. I simply sat for the first few years. I danced with my flags during worship, but I did not actively serve. In fact, I actually decided that teaching/preaching was no longer my thing. I focussed solely on the dance ministry, which I thoroughly enjoyed. Although the dance ministry was an independent group outside of my own church, my leaders were in support of it.

I can remember having coffee with my new Pastors and talking generally about life. During this conversation they asked me some very pertinent questions something along the lines of; "What do you need from us?" and "How can we support you?" To me that moment will forever be a mental marker for servant leadership. I felt like this was the very first time I had been asked these questions by a church leader. 'How can we help you?' It was usually the other way around, meaning that leaders wanted to know how you could help them. How you could serve; how you could give, and the list goes on. This was monumental, and my value and "commitment to the church" was never questioned because I did not serve in any capacity. I was afforded the space and time to heal. The leadership at my new church were aware of the gift of God on the inside of me; but there is sometimes a level of brokenness that does not allow for effective service. At this point the most important factor is for such individuals to be healed.

Those who have experienced spiritual abuse often need healing, deliverance and restoration. There is no need to apologise for taking the time needed to receive what you need.

It was during a conversation with my new pastor, in which I shared some of what I had previously experienced at Eden House. He then went on to explain that what I had been through was in fact spiritual abuse! This was news to me. But I now had language to explain what had happened. As I began to research and read around this subject, it all began to make sense and I was now better able to see exactly what I needed healing from.

As part of the dance ministry I was visiting other churches locally and one day one of the ministers from another church rang to speak to me about an upcoming event. Part way through the conversation he said, "I know you dance Fran, but I believe there is more in you and I would love for you to speak at our youth conference." >sigh< I was overwhelmed and in that moment the shadow and sting of my old pastor's words that, "who would ask you to speak again" was lifted. No more hiding; no more choosing to believe I could not speak, no more living under a lie. Freedom had come. Since that time, I have been sharing and regularly speaking at my own church, and at other churches on occasion too.

I will forever be grateful for those few years that I sat and was allowed to just be. I did not know that I needed to unlearn and relearn that my value and worth is found in Christ, not in how much I served. It taught me that service to God, through ministry of any sort to His people is a choice and an honour. That this cannot be, neither should be demanded. It taught me that even though I may not be openly serving in church for a season, Gods love for me remains intact. It also taught me that God is just as pleased with me. He does not need me to "perform" for an applaud, affirmation or praise. If this resonates with you, please know that you can serve or not serve in church and God still loves you. You have value and worth. You are part of the body and your gift of service is for a time, a season and a particular people who will gratefully receive it. Gods desire is that we willingly serve in obedience to Him, with no strings attached.

◆ Church Finances

Money, money, money! It is the root of all evil right? No! It is the love of money wherein lies the problem! 1 Timothy 6:10 teaches:

> *For the love of money is a root of all kinds of evil, for which some have strayed from the faith in their greediness, and pierced themselves through with many sorrows.*

> 1 Timothy 6:10 NKJV

I would argue that over the last few decades, the 'love of money' is how many churches have been operating. The era of the 'prosperity gospel' has taught us that to be wealthy or to receive financial blessing is in itself a manifestation of God's blessing. Conversely, not to have financial wealth must mean that there is something wrong with you and you are possibly suffering from the 'curse of poverty.' I will not start a theoretical debate on this subject here; however, one of the areas that I had to be healed from was my distorted relationship about faith and finance.

Whilst at Eden House, I had seen and participated in altar calls, often these huge theatrical displays during which you were invited to place your financial 'gift'…'seed' or 'sacrifice' at the altar; along with your tithes and offerings. I had often seen this charade at large 'evangelical' events and also on Christian TV shows. The "sow $100 for your 100-day miracle" request, and it was very concerning. It is like the classic 'sow into the church roof fund' request, that goes on for years and years, yet the church roof never materialises. Furthermore, no one was ever really sure what happened to the raised funds. I believed this was what happened in the majority of churches.

It was several months after being at my new church, that I came to an interesting realisation. I observed and was incredibly shocked that I had not 'yet' heard them preach on giving tithes and offerings. The leaders had not 'yet' made it a subject of 'do this and God will bless you.' The leaders had not 'yet' asked the congregation to sow into this anointing or sow into that miracle. In spite of these 'requests' not being evangelically demanded from the pulpit, people in the church willingly gave. The practice of tithing, giving offerings and also sowing financial seed are biblical principles. I wholeheartedly believe in doing so. To now find myself in an environment where I could freely give finances was liberating. We were taught on Biblical finances, but it was never coupled with a 'spiritual threat' of what is or is not going to happen, as a consequence of non-compliance. I recall sitting in a church Annual General Meeting (AGM) and the church treasurer going through the yearly financial reports. I was amazed at how financially secure the church was, despite no one being asked to give specific amounts at certain times of the year. This church was financially secure, despite the fact that there was not a succession of visiting preachers being allowed to coerce the congregation to part with their money in the following manner: "There are 10 of you in the congregation who need to sow $1000 ... its OK, I'll wait for you .... You know you've got it ... you know God is going to do a miracle for you, if you will just run to the front right now ... it's OK if you haven't got your cheque book .... You can pledge it ... its OK ... yes, I see you, there are 10 of you still sat down ... stop fighting it ... this is your time ... if you haven't got cash you can use a credit card ... just sow into this anointing!" Then after a few minutes the next level of givers would be summoned. "OK, so for those of you who can sow $500 this is your time ... I see you coming ... thank you ... yes, if you can't pay till next month, just pledge it ... God needs your seed ... there are still 20 of you that need to sow $500 ..." and so it would go on; $250, $100, $50 etc. The church was financially secure without any of these unbiblical 'tactics.'

If hearing this type of talk from the pulpit make you feel uncomfortable, it is a good thing. There are so many others who have been conditioned that this type of financial manipulation is normal; that this is right and that this is acceptable. I do not see any scriptural basis for this type of coercion to give. Believers are invited to give financially, but to give from a willing heart. We are not to give from a place of fear, based on what we think might happen if we do not give. The fear that a particular 'curse' will not be broken off from your life, if you are unable to meet their standards of financial given.

The handling of church finances and the complete absence of a command to sow for 'abc' has helped to heal my beliefs concerning giving. It has helped to teach me a new and better pattern. I now understand that there can be an honest, open and transparent honour culture in church when it comes to finances. I am now free to choose to give, as I am giving to the Lord from a willing heart.

Two things that really disturbs me about the financial area of spiritual abuse is that it is both manipulative and deceptive. If your church needs money, morally, it may be better just to be upfront and explain that you are fundraising for 'xyz' project. Simply ASK if people are in a financial position to help, or if they would like to! The second disturbing factor is that vulnerable individuals are cajoled into going into debt to pay a 'seed' to receive a blessing that was already theirs in the first place. It was already theirs because of the finished work of the Cross.

Beloved, you are free to give. You are loved, blessed and cherished no matter the amount you give. There are genuine leaders and shepherds who do not fleece their sheep for monetary gain. There are genuine leaders and shepherds who do not allow hireling shepherds access to the sheep, just so that they too can play their part in this catastrophic financial theatrical drama.

✦ Healthy Relationships Within The Church

God created us to be relational beings. To relate, commune, fellowship and interact with other people. The impact of spiritual abuse can have a devastating effect on relationships. This is because often the very people that we were created to live in community with, relate to, and have fellowship with, have often been the greatest source of our pain. Interestingly, it is also people that the Lord will use to be a catalyst for parts of our healing journey. I personally used to be very naïve. I used to believe what most people said, especially leaders. I used to believe that most people were good. That because someone had a title, this actually meant something. I thought it meant that they were honest, trustworthy and responsible. I have since learnt that character is far more important than titles, anointing and accolades. That respect is a two-way thing and should always be reciprocal.

I also had a serious issue with trust. On hindsight, I was on one hand, way too trusting at times, and then on the other hand, I would go in completely the opposite direction and not trust at all. The revelation that I had been in a spiritually abusive environment, had really caused me to wonder if there were actually any genuine people. Genuine people who were not focussed purely on what they could get out of me. Long held, deeply ingrained beliefs, can at times take longer to be completely changed. It takes a conscious effort not to be cynical and deem someone untrustworthy, simply because of our past experiences. Just remember that healing is a process. Discernment and wisdom are essential when cultivating healthy interactions and relationships with others. If your involvement in church activities is cloaked in secrecy, then this may be an indication that there is something amiss. Genuine relationships require transparency.

Along with this truth, I had to unlearn and relearn that you cannot judge a church solely based on its appearance. There was an elitist culture in Eden House that pretty much said, "no other church is as good as our church ... where can you go and get healed, delivered and receive a miracle!" The anointing, if genuine, is the Spirit of God operating within an individual. Therefore, no man can take credit for it. Whilst the anointing is great, in dealing with others character is very important. We are called to have the character of Christ.

In Matthew 7:21-23 Jesus taught:

> *Not everyone who says to Me, 'Lord, Lord,' shall enter the kingdom of heaven, but he who does the will of My Father in heaven. Many will say to Me in that day, 'Lord, Lord, have we not prophesied in Your name, cast out demons in Your name, and done many wonders in Your name?' And then I will declare to them, 'I never knew you; depart from Me, you who practice lawlessness!*
>
> Matthew 7:21-23 NKJV

This word is sobering, but be encouraged. There are children of God who demonstrate Christ's image, character and likeness. They are trustworthy and genuine. I pray your heart would be healed enough to discern, believe and accept these Christ like people when they show up in your life. I can testify that healthy and wholesome relationships are a powerful source of healing.

◆ My Ability To Hear From God

My ability to hear God for my own life was negatively impacted by being in a spiritually abusive environment. In a spiritually abusive environment one of the most commonly held beliefs is that the leader has this superhuman, almost magical, completely exclusive ability to hear from God. Not only for the church, but for your personal life; for the decisions you should make, what you should and should not do! The belief is that the prophetic unction is only for the leaders, Gods specially chosen and anointed vessels. As such the congregation has an indispensable need for the leaders. It is as though they were the only gateway to God. Although not often spoken directly, but more often than not implied, that you have to go through them to get to God. After all, how would God speak to little 'ol me directly. Lies !! It is not true, and I know that for a while my confidence and understanding that God speaks to me directly about my life, was badly dented. To be more acurate, it was severely damaged.

The lack of confidence caused me to become uncertain of my ability to make choices, and decisions without a number of confirmations or prophecies. When that was not available I looked to family and close friends to help me get to a decision; desperately needing their approval, about my own life! This is something that only became apparent in the latter years of my healing journey, as I began to recognise the root cause. There was a fear of 'getting it wrong.' You need to know that God is a good father, and that He desires us to talk to Him and also listen, as we are led by the Holy Spirit. Of course our leaders can speak a word into our lives, but beloved please know that God can speak to you directly.

He can speak in many ways, and not having a title does not disqualify you hearing Him. One of the main ways God speaks to us is through His word, the Bible. One thing I am continually learning is that you should always obey what God is calling you to do. It is a beautiful thing when your dependency is on Him.

Beloved, I repeat, you can hear from God for yourself. Your past, even your past mistakes do not disqualify you from hearing God.

♦ A Changing Perspective On Church Culture

There were other aspects of church life that I had to unlearn, and my new church provided the scope for those lessons to take place. It was as though God would strategically 'set-up' situations so I could observe what I needed to learn, in order to develop a new perspective on the church. There were far too many situations for me to detail here. As I mentioned previously, I believe each of our journey towards healing will look different; because we each have different sized and different shaped emotional and mental wounds.

The very first evening service I attended at my new church, I can recall sitting at the very back of the building. It was from this position that I could quickly reach the door if I needed to make a swift exit. What precisely I thought would happen, I wasn't sure, but remember I had trust issues, plus serious levels of scepticism. So, I was tentatively participating in the service, and we were at the point where the preaching had started. I noticed an older, poorly dressed man wandered into the church. He looked like he was having a rough day and he looked like he smelt of unwashed clothes and alcohol. At first this man sat down and was listening to the minister, then he got up. He got up in the middle of the preaching and started talking, and making a bit of a scene. I immediately started to feel nervous and mildly anxious. In a split second my mind went back to Eden House, and I was anticipating the same kind of response to a 'situation' like this. In Eden House ushers would be summoned by a leader to "get that person out of the building."After which they would very swiftly and not at all lovingly be escorted from the building. But here I was in this new place, and I was expecting the same thing to happen. Would this man get violent? Would there be a big scene? The ushers weren't obviously identifiable as they weren't wearing uniforms. But then something very unexpected happened. I mean, really unexpected. Here I was bracing myself for a confrontational scene, but yet this man was confronted in a very different way.

The man stood up, and was still talking. He had started walking to the front of the church. He was talking directly at the minister who was preaching, in an accusing manner. Rather than reacting as I would have anticipated, the minister stopped preaching. He walked down from the pulpit to meet the man in the aisle and began ministering and speaking with him directly. I was confused. Here was the preacher, taking time out from his preaching to minister to this poorly dressed man. This is what Jesus would have done. I had never witnessed this before. After a few minutes the man was asked to take a seat, which he did willingly, and the usher sat next to him. Immediately after service someone gave him a cup of tea and biscuits.

I had not experienced leadership like this. Loving, kind, no agenda, no anger at the disruption of their message. Jesus left the ninety-nine for the one. The one matters to Him; so surely the one should matter to pastors and leaders too.

What did not happen very often at my new church, especially after the first year of me attending, was the obligatory altar call at the end of every service. At the end of service when the Pastor would pray, instead he would often say "the chair is your altar!!' At first I was so confused by this. I asked myself why wasn't a public altar call made; why weren't those who needed ministry invited to the front, so that we could all see and celebrate the anointing; the move of God, the deliverance and healing etc.

It felt so unfamiliar for the 'show' not to be so public. It was strange that we were encouraged to pray for ourselves, lay hands on ourselves and pray by ourselves. Personal ministry was always available for those who needed it, but there was an intentionality about going to and growing in God for ourselves! It was strangely refreshing that this was encouraged, and not total dependence of the pastors being the 'gateway to God'. It also meant taking responsibility and not being lazy or passive in regards to always receiving ministry. After all, going up for prayer, falling down at the altar, and getting back up week after week is not always the thing that brings about the changes that are necessary for our spiritual growth and development.

The church and church leadership were also very down to earth. There was no divisive hierarchy, that meant this one or that one was pandered to because of a role, title or position they fulfilled. There were no special, better than everyone else's chairs designated only for the pastors and the ministers, that no 'common' person ever dare sit upon! As simple as it may seem, in my mind, this implied that there was a culture that demonstrated, we are all one body. Each with a valuable role to play. The pastors and leaders did not require, expect or demand to be pandered to, but they led with integrity and were still greatly respected. The love and mutual respect was evident and there wasn't a hint of leadership elitism. In fact, I recall one leader who I noticed often came to church wearing a casual tracksuit. This did not fit in to my notion of church attire. I believed then, that a leader should be suited and booted to lead in church. I reserved my thoughts to myself, but I did think it strange. Then one day this leader was testifying that the Lord had told her to come to church in a tracksuit and trainers; so that if a visitor who came for the first time, was also in a tracksuit and trainers they would not feel out of place. This challenged my thinking, and I came to the realisation that what I believe to be the right way, is not always so.

I love this scripture in Isaiah:

> *For as the heavens are higher than the earth, So are My ways higher than your ways, And My thoughts than your thoughts."*

Isaiah 55:9 NKJV

We cannot and should not ever try to put God in a box, according to our thinking or our experiences. I was unlearning and relearning what a different model of leadership in the church and the church culture could look like. I was beginning to like it.

CHAPTER TEN

The Purpose Picture

"Purpose unfolds like a scroll in your lifetime"

Pastor Michael Ekwulugo

*I*magine, a beautifully intrinsically designed pattern of bricks on the floor. A masterful mosaic created from individual bricks. Picture the scene, the creator, designer and orchestrator of the puzzle looking over their work. Whilst each individual brick was aesthetically pleasing, its real beauty was seen when the first brick was pushed and set in place alongside the one next to it. Then the next and then the next … some bricks were connected to several and they in turn had a massive impact. The sound of connecting, the sound of movement and the sound of impact. Although each brick stood alone, it was created to connect and have impact on others. Together the masterpiece was created.

A bit like bricks, but more significantly, you and I have been designed to connect and impact others. 1 Corinthians 12 speaks about believers being part of the 'body'. I love how the Bible describes that "the foot cannot say to the hand I have no need of you" because each part is important. To each survivor of spiritual abuse, I need to remind you that you have a place; a position, a purpose for being born at this time and in this generation. Where you were born was not by chance or accident, there is a reason behind it. Your life has meaning. Your life matters.

One of the lasting impacts of spiritual abuse, beyond the damage, that we discussed in earlier chapters, is the misalignment of individuals. They are often no longer positioned in their rightful place. Their gifting, anointing and character are no longer serving the kingdom, impacting, or influencing others. Similarly, when one part of the physical body is misaligned, broken or missing the rest of the body feels it. Whilst other parts of the body can compensate and 'help out' it is not quite the same and it can cause pressure, tension and imbalance.

Each of us have been created uniquely, and what we share and bring to the table is different. Whilst we can have similarities, likes, or share common traits with other people, we can never be duplicated entirely. The damage goes beyond the individual survivor, and reaches to the very souls they were destined to impact. The Bible says we do not wrestle against flesh and blood. Therefore, we can understand that what has happened to a survivor of spiritual abuse was perhaps part of a demonic strategy to hinder them in their calling and anointing. It is like a skilled saboteur, who will identify and target those who have great potential. There is often a pattern in the lives of those who have experienced spiritual abuse. They often have a strong calling on their life, or to break down the *Christianese*, as my Pastor, would say, they were born to do something incredible in this world.

Imagine where we would be, if we had not experienced all that we went through. Or even if we had not experienced it for so long. What might we have accomplished; what might we be doing, where might we be serving more effectively?

Jesus is the greatest redeemer. I have faith to believe that lost time will never be an obstacle to that which you were destined to accomplish for the kingdom. What you were destined to achieve in five years, God can equip you to achieve in two years, as you put your trust in Him. The people and places that you were meant to reach in two years could be reached in one. Do not allow the enemy to whisper the lie that it is too late, and that you have missed it.

Bending Time (Accessing Heavenly Realities for Abundant Living) was a book that opened my eyes on the concept of Kairos time. May I paraphrase an encouragement from this book:

"Time is your servant. You are the perfect age for everything that God has for you right now. Time will make room for the purpose of God to be fulfilled in your life and in your generation."

Your healing and restoration is to serve a purpose greater than you. It is for the kingdom.

CONCLUSION

*S*piritual abuse is not an easy subject, and in the words of my Pastor, "spiritual abuse is perhaps one of the worst forms of abuse, because it isn't often recognised for what it is, and it is quite 'normalised' in many church circles."

Spiritual abuse, like many other forms of abuse is a complex matter. The incidents involved are often intertwined with other regular "normal" interactions, communication and behaviour. This, for the survivor, can sometimes be a source of confusion. The perpetrators and key people involved may often be charismatic, gifted and helpful. They may even be great orators with the capability of drawing a crowd. They can appear charming and personable, and are sometimes likable to the masses. There are times when survivors of spiritual abuse experience their good side and good interactions. Their laughter, smiles and care. This may leave survivors in conflict, as they wonder whether their bad experiences were really that bad after all.

It is often not true that the perpetrators inflict their abusive behaviour on everyone. This can therefore make the survivors stories seem unbelievable to the outsider who may only see their 'good side.'

In spite of the confusing and mixed thoughts, feelings and emotions the truth is the truth. Jesus is the way, the truth and the life. He is the measuring line by which we compare conduct.

Manipulation, control and all forms of spiritual abuse and mistreatment are not the Biblical pattern that we ought to live by.

I do think it necessary to make it clear that not all leaders are spiritually abusive, even though many leaders can come across as strong and authoritative. Leaders have a responsibility to take care of their 'flock' and at times this may mean sharing harsh truths. Harsh only because we do not want to hear it. Leaders may rebuke your behaviour or speech and seek to correct wrong thinking, all of which is Biblical. However, the place from which this should be done is love. Leaders should be driven by the Spirit of God, to nurture and care for their 'sheep.' Desiring that they become more Christ like, and deepen their walk with Him, so they are destined for an eternity in God's presence.

This has been a story of hope, healing and restoration in and through Christ. May that be the fragrance that you are left with; may this book serve as a reminder that a joy filled life can be found after brokenness. That purpose can be realised after pain

This has truly been a labour of love, and whilst writing I have thought and felt many things. I in no way consider myself an expert in the area of spiritual abuse, neither am I a theologian or have all the answers. This has been me sharing my story, not an in depth study of this subject. As such there may be many other components of this topic that you felt have not been covered. I whole heartedly agree and would encourage those with a passion to also write, share, encourage and teach and so further the healing for the brokenness caused by spiritual abuse.

My hope and prayer is simply that heaven is pleased with what you hold in your hand, as testament to my obedience to the Lords leading. My hope and prayer is that this book has in some way been helpful.

I am healed, I am whole. I love Jesus, I love His church. I love leadership. I am a leader. Forgiveness was fundamental to my freedom. I have forgiven all those who caused me hurt and harm, and I pray for them.

I am living in the purpose God set for me; I have been restored and I know I have an incredible future ahead of me.

At the end of this book you will find a letter to other survivors of spiritual abuse. A letter to those who may have a loved one in a spiritually abusive environment and a letter to leaders.

Thank you being a part of this journey.

A Letter To Survivors

Beloved,

I dedicated this book to you. I celebrate your life because despite being hurt, neglected and rejected, your resilience, tenacity and inner determination to survive is phenomenal. Healing and wholeness in and through Jesus are woven into your destiny.

Whether what you have been through has been recognised, acknowledged or not, I encourage you with the truth that you matter. Your story matters. Whether you share it or not the Lord Himself has seen it all. If you have not yet shared, you may need to unburden that story if it still weighs heavy on your heart. Healing is possible, peace is available and hope can be yours.

My prayer for you is that any identity that is not yours will be stripped away.

Remember:

- You are not what happened to you.

- You are not what was said to you, that did not align with Gods truth.

- You are not your failure, mistake or wrongs. That simply makes you human.

- You are not your pain and brokenness.

- ◆ You are not a powerless victim

I pray that you would have the revelation that you are free to live solely in the identity, acceptance and love of Christ and your stature in Him. And choose that to be the narrative and navigating anchor of your life.

No matter where you are on your healing journey, do not be afraid to ask, accept and receive help and support.

It is perfectly acceptable to have counselling or therapy as a believer; Jesus heals in many ways.

Lastly Psalm 139 says you are fearfully and wonderfully made – may you be soaked and saturated in these scriptural truths. I'm praying for you,

Blessings.

The following prayer is for those who have walked away from God because of hurt and wounded-ness.

Dear Heavenly Father,

I thank you that Jesus died, in order that I might live. I bring before You every single thing that I have been through and lay it all your feet. I bring every hurt, every wound, every deep and buried thing that still causes me pain. Every question, every concern and every ounce of confusion. I choose to forgive all those that hurt me. I desire to be healed and made whole, I do not know how to make this happen, but I know that You do. I recommit my life to you; I believe and confess that Jesus is my Lord and Saviour. For any wrong that I have done I now ask for your forgiveness. I am sorry for seeing the behaviour and actions of others and blaming you. I am sorry for partnering with the pain and growing a hard heart. I am sorry for building a wall that was meant to keep others out, but inadvertently kept you out also. I am ready to process the pain, and receive the complete healing and restoration you have provided.

Thank you for loving me, as no one else could. You are my Father and I am your child. I now choose life; I now choose freedom in Christ.

In Jesus name

Amen

Letter To Those With A Loved One Who May Have Or Are Experiencing Spiritual Abuse

Dearest,

If you are the loved one of someone who you suspect or believe is in a spiritually abusive or toxic environment, remain loving and supportive. Remember, they may not know that they are there in that kind of place. If they do have concerns, they may not want to fully believe them at this point, or acknowledge the concerns you raise. There may be fear, denial and a range of other mixed emotions. Put this book in their hand – continue to pray and lovingly support them. Remind them that you will always be there for them. Many times they will be under a cloud of deception and may not know what they are in, so do not condemn them. I remember after leaving Eden House and bumping into an old leader who had also left the church sometime before me. I was taken aback when she said that her and a few others had been praying for years that my eyes would be opened and I would be able to 'get out!'

Being in a spiritually abusive environment often impacts an individual's sub conscious mental faculty. It changes the make-up of their structure, their emotional and mental DNA. Figuratively, not literally. Experiences of spiritual abuse can distort, cloud and significantly colour an individual's perspective. Your loved one may be ultra-sensitive and easily offended, as what is often said differs from what they 'perceived' was said.

Leaving a church, organisation or relationship you've been part of for years is a type of loss. For some it may even feel like a death. It takes incredible strength and courage to make that decision, and then follow through with that decision. For many, like myself, leaving church also meant that within a year I lost those I had considered family, I lost my social life, my support system, my role, my ministry and regular contact with people I was connected to. They may go through a season of mourning and grieving ... yes, even though it was toxic, there were still real relationships that have now ended. I recall feeling liberated after I left, but also scared as I had never known adulthood without Eden House being such a central and important part of my life. I had so much extra time on my hands, as church commitments no longer caused me to be busy for the majority of the week. However, I still felt lost. It took me months to stabilise, and get used to being by myself so much more. I was fortunate to still have a few supportive and nurturing relationships, through which agape (love) was poured out. I had loved ones regularly praying for me and I will forever be grateful that God provided that which I did not know I needed.

He who the Son sets free is free indeed. Truth.

Your loved one may not want or be ready to talk about what they may have experienced, so be patient. They may also not want to talk about it with you, and I would encourage you not to take it personally. I remember that some loved ones would not, in my view, almost want to believe some of what I was sharing about my experiences. Partly because their experience and memory of key individuals was so different, and they had only ever seen the 'nice, charming' side. But also because it is painful, and no one wants to think about what their loved one went through. In this way it can feel easier to disbelieve it, rather than have to process it. Maybe you, yourself, will need to talk to someone after hearing some of their stories and experiences. And it can take time, months, possibly years for your loved ones to share everything. Trauma has a way of affecting the brain, memory and the recollection of past experiences. It can be years after when a fresh memory is brought to the surface as and when the individual is able to process it in a safe way. Your loved one may also be 'triggered' in unexpected ways, so stay supportive and be understanding. It is a journey, but there is light along the journey and at the end of the tunnel.

Jesus is the Way, Truth and the Life.

Healing and restoration is possible. I am praying for you all.

Your sister in Christ.

Letter To Leaders

Dear leaders,

To lead is to serve, to lead is to submit, to lead is to support. To be a leader is such an honourable position, to be entrusted to support others is a privilege and should be treated with respect. If after reading this book, you have discovered that you have been guilty of spiritual abuse, I encourage you to ask for forgiveness and repent, to change your ways. I encourage you to seek Godly wise counsel and also apologise to those who you may have hurt. It takes humility and courage to apologise, and depending on the extent of the abuse further decisions may need to be taken. I believe healing, restoration and deliverance are available, but for some the right next step may be to step down from leading.

For leaders of leaders I encourage you to open up this topic, to cultivate a culture of both support and healthy challenge amongst each other. To create an environment where we check on each other, check on motives, check on our own issues in order to safeguard each other. Leaders are human and imperfect and we accept that; but there is an expectation that leaders lead with integrity, with humility and remain teachable.

There is support available, and I know there is hope for redemption. Jesus is our greatest example of leadership. He laid His life down for people, for us, our needs He esteemed greater than His own comfort.

I believe leadership was given by God for a purpose and leadership is a powerful tool that can harm but can also heal.

May we all adopt, actualise and avail ourselves to be servant leaders and remain accountable.

I am praying for you.

Signs of Spiritual Abuse

There are various situations, factors and scenarios that would demonstrate that someone is experiencing spiritual abuse or is in a spiritually abusive and toxic environment. It may be that several people are in the same church, but they may not all experience, if at all, spiritual abuse in the same way. As such it would not be wise to produce a tick list. When a believer has discernment and is accountable I believe Holy Spirit can reveal and prompt when "something isn't quite right".

This list is not comprehensive and there could be many other behaviour indicators that would evidence that you, or someone you know has, or still is experiencing spiritual abuse.

However, as deception and dis-empowerment can work as twin terrors, it may be helpful to read the list, and share with someone that you trust, and talk through any concerns or questions that may arise from this list. There is wisdom in godly counsel, and a support network is vitally necessary when you start the journey to freedom.

35 Signs of Spiritually Abusive Leadership And Environments

These toxic behaviours may be found in the church community generally, or may just relate to one or two leaders.

1. They are verbally abusive, using intimidating language and threats.

2. They openly or coercively control what people do and the decisions they make.

3. Any and all sexual abuse, including inappropriate touch, comments and advances.

4. They are manipulative and play on people's emotions to get what they want.

5. A lot of meetings and discussions are held in secret, and you are asked to keep secrets.

6. They pitch the leaders/members against one another by comparing and speaking about them in a derogatory way

7. They use bribery and finances as a way to 'secure' God's blessings.

8. They make everything about them, their image, their ego and their name.

9. They see the congregation as solely there to serve them.

10. They claim they are above reproach.

11. They oppose accountability and do not hold themselves accountable to anyone.

12. They threaten to curse members, if you leave their church.

13. They berate the congregation for what they may lack spiritually or materially.

14. They forbid their congregation from visiting other churches.

15. They expect an unreasonable level of commitment to the church, which can feel like the members are in a 'covenant'.

16. They use fear as form of control.

17. They have an elitist approach to leadership and church governance.

18. 'Favour' is given to the most compliant members.

19. The bigger financial givers are afforded privileges.

20. Rather than truth and transparency, there is a culture of lies and deceit.

21. Members are made an example of publicly.

22. Love is conditional based on one's ability to give and serve

23. They invite other ministers to manipulate the congregation into financial giving.

24. They show favour to the wealthy or those that can benefit the church because of their social status.

25. They use the word of God to manipulate the congregation for personal and financial gain.

26. They discourage close relationships with family members and others who are not in their particular church.

27. They place a high demand on member's time, implying that all other activities outside of the church are unimportant, unnecessary and ungodly.

28. Some would encourage members to leave an unsaved spouse.

29. They imply that only they have the ability to hear revelations from God.

30. Titles are very important.

31. There is a mixture of the sacred and the profane.

32. There is a preference for cultural practices over the kingdom requirement.

33. They call you a witch or a Jezebel if you disagree.

34. They dissuade fellowship with members outside of their control

35. A person's character is rarely taken into account if it benefits the church.

Some would argue that this list is more akin to practices you find in a 'cult' rather than a church setting. Again I would strongly implore you to seek godly counsel, if you recognise any these behaviours or patterns.

Further Resources

Visit **www.survivingspiritualabuse.com** for resources, links to Christian counsellors and the ReStart Coaching programmes specifically designed to support survivors and leaders.

Join our community on Facebook and Instagram **@ssa.restart**

Email: info@survivingspiritualabuse.com

Further reading

The Subtle Power of Spiritual Abuse by David Johnson and Jeff Vab Vonderen

Savage Shepherds by Adam Harbinson

Toxic Faith by Stephen Arterburn and Jack Felton

Broken Trust by F. Remy Diederich

Healing Spiritual Abuse by Ken Blue

Bending Time by Dan McCollam

Francesca McDowall is a Leadership and Life Coach committed to working with individuals and organisations to find and fulfil their purpose. She holds a MA in Coaching & Mentoring, a BSc in Psychology, is a Public Speaker and also an Award Winning Mentor. Francesca loves Jesus and serves in her local church in the West Midlands, UK.

OTHER BOOKS BY THE AUTHOR

Women Who Win (*For Women Who Are Ready To Turn Their Pain Into Purpose And Their Purpose Into Profit*).

By Simone Bell & Francesca McDowall

Are you tired of feeling like you always settle for less in life? Are you fed up of living a monotonous, mundane and mediocre life? Do you know you are destined for more than what you currently have and are experiencing? If any of this sounds familiar this book Women Who Win was written just for you. Amongst other things this book will teach you:

♦ The importance of discovering and walking in your purpose.

♦ Why your personal story is crucial to your success.

♦ Why goal setting in and of itself is not enough.

♦ How to present with confidence formally and informally.

♦ How to increase your business credibility.

♦ How to improve your personal relationship with money.

119 Tips For Public Speaking

By Adam Butler & Francesca McDowall

Do you have a speaking engagement, an interview, a podcast, or any

other kind of speech coming up? Do you start shaking and sweating at the very thought of it? Don't worry this is the place to start. This book isn't intended only for people taking the stage; it's for anybody that wants to be heard, seen and connected with. Whether you work through the book page by page or just take occasional tips ...This book will help you achieve confidence and deliver the talk of your life.

Dear reader/writer,

*I would like to take this opportunity to thank you for supporting **one** of our newest authors.*

Here at Open Scroll Publications, we specialise in assisting talented writers to fulfil their dreams and aspirations. The creative process is hard enough as it is without having to worry about getting your masterpiece published once you're finally done. That's why Open Scroll Publications was formed. We demystify the process of getting published, and give a literary voice to those who would otherwise be muted in obscurity.

Our list of gifted writers is rapidly growing, and I would like to invite you to consider becoming our next distinguished author. So, whether you're working on a novel, a children's book, a poetry anthology, or an inspirational non-fiction piece, why not take a leap of faith and contact us? We would love to hear from you.

For more information, please visit us at:
www.openscroll.co.uk
info@openscroll.co.uk
Phone: 01213502422
         07506677504

Or write to us at:
Open Scroll Publications Ltd,
Kemp House,
160 City Road,
London, EC1V 2NX.

Made in the USA
Middletown, DE
04 September 2021